GRANDAD'S A

Michael Franckeiss

ARTHUR H. STOCKWELL LTD.
Elms Court   Ilfracombe   Devon
Established 1898

© Michael Franckeiss, 1998
First published in Great Britain, 1998
All rights reserved.
No part of this publication may be reproduced
or transmitted in any form or by any means,
electronic or mechanical, including photocopy,
recording, or any information storage and
retrieval system, without permission
in writing from the copyright holder.

British Library Cataloguing-in-Publication Data.
A catalogue record for this book is available
from the British Library.

By the same author:
I Never Cried

Cover photo:– *Ready for action, Innsworth, 1951*

ISBN 0 7223 3188-6
*Printed in Great Britain by
Arthur H. Stockwell Ltd.
Elms Court   Ilfracombe
Devon*

CONTENTS

Introduction	5
Victoria Hall, Portsmouth	7
A Little Background	10
To Padgate	12
At Padgate	14
Posted to Innsworth	18
At RAF Innsworth	20
Pool Flight	31
RAF Hednesford	34
To RAF Wharton and Back	37
Hednesford Again	39
Hitchhiking	41
Break-in	44
A Posh Friend	47
Brass Monkeys	49
Me and the Sarge, and Jankers	51
No Mean Feat	52
Sport and Sour Grapes	54
Cranwell	56
Is a 48-hour Pass Worth a Bollocking?	59
Skeggy	61
Hednesford and Porton Down	63
RAF Debden	66
Promotion	71
In at the Deep End	72
Officers' Ladies	74
Commitment	76
Close Encounters of the Wrong Kind	78
Right Marker	80
Into Battle	82
Let Me Out	84
Demob at Last	87

Dedications
AC2 2515786 M. P. Franckeiss:

To the other two million, five hundred and fifteen thousand, seven hundred and eighty-five airmen before me.

To my parents and my wife's parents, for their help during my National Service.

Many thanks to David for converting my long hand into type.

INTRODUCTION

It is more than likely that many Grandads like me would have been asked by the their grandchildren what it was like doing National Service. I can truthfully say that I had an easy time, and the main reason for this was the job I was in which, to give it its real title, was batman/waiter, but to a good many people I was an officer's flunky.

I could put up with the ridicule, after all I always had the last laugh when it came to guard duties, fire picket, parades, etc. They were duties almost unknown to me during my Service time.

The food that I was eating in the officers' mess was far superior to the food which was dished up in the airmen's mess. Another plus!! My quarters in the mess were very comfortable, and I had no need to venture out in inclement weather to reach my place of work, and, unlike many National Servicemen, I would never have to fire a gun in anger.

Many books have been written about this period of our history, so just let me say that this narrative is an absolutely true account of my time in the Royal Air Force, and it pleases me to think that maybe my grandchildren's children will one day read this, even though I was only an officer's flunky!! I feel sure that they will have some pleasure out of reading this little piece of history, and I sincerely hope "dear reader" that you too will gain some pleasure and amusement at my effort with the pen.

VICTORIA HALL, PORTSMOUTH

It came through the letter box on 16th January, a buff-coloured envelope addressed to yours truly. All was revealed on opening the envelope with OHMS in one corner. "I wonder what it is?" I should have known. *Report with this letter to your Labour Exchange, at once.* And so it was Lake Road here I come.

As is so common with these places, I had to wait for my turn at the window.

"How can I help you?"

It was my turn at last. "This letter came for me yesterday." My first mistake. What I should have said was "This letter came today." I handed the letter to an outstretched hand.

"Ah, yes, call-up papers. Why didn't you come at once as directed?"

"I had to go to work; it was important to the firm's customer."

The gent at the window did not seem very impressed with my answer. "Oh" was all he said, but I am sure he did not believe me. "Did you bring your birth certificate?" he asked, and I feel sure he expected a negative reply. I handed him the document.

"Yes, that seems in order Mr Franckeiss, now would you wait a few moments and I will arrange a time for you to report to Victoria Hall."

Victoria Hall was the venue for my medical. The gent at the Labour Exchange arranged the time and date. I suppose it didn't occur to him to ask if these times were suitable from my point of view. "You must keep this appointment" he stressed.

My appointment was to be the next day at 11 a.m. "How long will it take?" I asked him.

"How dare you ask me that, I have no idea. I only work in one office at a time" he replied.

I did wonder what side of the bed he got out of; he was such a misery guts!! I needed to know the length of time it would take. That would be the question my employer would ask.

Well, the interview with this "civil" servant came to an end, but there was still more verbal diarrhoea to come; this time from my governor. "They can't do this. Who do they think they are? I have made arrangements for tomorrow, now look what you have done" was what he said.

By this time I had had enough of this treatment. "Don't blame me, I am only doing what thousands of people my age are doing and that is what I have been ordered to do. You get on to the Labour Exchange, not me" I said.

Surprised I was to hear my governor apologise. "Sorry Mick, it's not your fault. You will be the fourth workman I have lost through National Service in the last nine months and I am bloody fed up with it" he replied.

So I reported to Victoria Hall on the 10th April in the morning for a medical; and a good medical it turned out to be. This was not one of those occasions of "Bend over; cough. OK. You are in".

I counted four doctors and they were all very thorough. I was one of a number of young men reporting for a National Service medical. Two or three of the people having their medicals, I recognised as old friends. One of these in particular had been a 'Mr South Coast Body-building Champion'. We were all told to remove our clothing, which we did, and we were all parading around to see different doctors with our "family jewels" swinging in the breeze!!

I never minded this at all, but for one thing, I tried my hardest not to stand next to 'Mr South Coast'. My body compared to his was quite inferior! Terry New was an ex-school chum of mine and I was pleased to see him, even if he did make me feel inferior!

As I have said, this was a real medical examination, and I did really want to be passed as fit. I had no inhibitions about doing my National Service. However, there was one cloud on the horizon; my eyesight was not spot on. This came as no surprise to me; I never did have perfect vision.

I was given an appointment to see an eye specialist in St Edwards Road in Southsea. This kind man asked me if I wanted to go into the Service, and my reply was yes. Somehow I had grown used to the idea. He gave me an envelope to hand back to the medical panel and once again I was asked to wait. It seemed that the result of my eye test was OK and I was given yet another form to complete. I was asked to present the form in person to the Victoria Hall Recruiting Office, which I did.

At the same time as presenting the eye test form, I was asked to fill in yet another form. This one was my preference for which Service; first, second and third choice; Army, Navy, Air Force. Hoping for the best I wrote Air Force in all three choices. I don't think this is what they wanted but I took the chance and it paid off!

An RAF sergeant gave me an aptitude test to complete. It must have been easy, I did it without any bother. I had to wait in a corridor outside the office of a flight lieutenant for an interview. I waited, and to keep warm I stood by a radiator. Probably without realising it I moved my hands, which were behind my back, in between the wall and the inside edge of the radiator.

After a boring thirty minutes, I was called into the office. The officer got to his feet and leaned over the desk, offering his hand. A nice gesture I thought, but, oh, calamity. The palms of my hands were covered with soot! I had been gathering this lovely black coating by running my hands along the back of the radiator whilst waiting for my interview. The officer's right hand became as black as mine. It was like a scene from that TV comedy "Some Mothers Do 'Ave 'Em". I apologised, of course, but what frightened me more than anything was the silence and the look of disdain on the officer's face. My first thoughts were 'Goodbye Air Force'.

My interview was fairly short. He did ask me if I would be interested in aircrew duties, but I knew my poor education would cancel that idea out. The interview came to an end and he bid me goodbye, but for some reason he didn't offer his hand.

I think like most people after an interview, you tend to think that it didn't go very well; in my case for one very good reason. He did say that I would be informed of the outcome of the interview in due course.

The wait was agonising. I waited for every post. At last, after about two weeks the all-important buff envelope arrived. I was given a date and time to report to RAF Padgate on the 4th May 1951, and also a railway warrant. So the officer had a sense of humour after all!

I must admit I was looking forward to giving my notice in. It was all a new adventure for me and I did look forward to donning the Air Force blue. As it happened a close friend of mine had his call-up papers, also for the Air Force, and fate would play a part in us meeting whilst serving!! But more of that later in the story.

A LITTLE BACKGROUND

Just a word or two about my life. I was six years old when World War Two began. In 1940 we were bombed out of our house in Cottage View, Portsmouth, and my parents took the decision to have me evacuated for safety. By this time I was seven years of age. I was evacuated to the New Forest; so for four years I was separated from my family. "So what" I hear you say, "so were thousands of others." I know this, of course, if you add these four years to the three I did in the Service, it amounted to seven years out of twenty-one that I was away from my home. You often read about wayward children who had their home lives disrupted for various reasons, and this excuse is used for their wayward behaviour more than anything. I think it is more like lack of strength of character. As I have said, the thought of doing my National Service gave me no reason to lose any sleep. I think I speak for a lot of people when I say that being separated from your social life was a bit of a wrench.

After leaving school at fourteen, I joined a youth club called Kingston Boys and was a founder member of Kangaroo Sports; mainly to follow my main interest, which was football. I played in the Lads' League and the Portsmouth North End League, and also Church's League. I have always considered that part of my life the most enjoyable.

The main venue after Saturday afternoon football, was to a dance on South Parade Pier, in Southsea, a lot of the time to see what "crumpet" was available.

As time drew near for me to leave home, I began to appreciate more the things I had taken for granted. A good home, a good mother and father and many friends, and in particular a lady who has been very kind to me in many ways in the latter part of World War Two.

I had packed my case and I had drawn the cash owed to me; my wages, holiday pay, and one week in hand — the wonderful sum of seven pounds! I felt quite rich. I had never saved money, so seven pounds was my worldly wealth. My father, true to form, offered me money, which I refused.

I don't remember sleeping the night before that eventful day I was due to leave home. I lived in Milton Road opposite Kingston Prison. My mother and father said goodbye to me on the doorstep. They wanted to come to the station but I asked them not to. My mother kissed me goodbye, a thing she did on only rare occasions.

TO PADGATE

I made my way to the bus stop to get to the Portsmouth town station, in time for the seven twenty-five to Waterloo. When I arrived at the upper level platform, quite a lot of people were waiting, but not to go to the train. They were there to say goodbye to two other young men who, as it happened, were reporting to RAF Padgate for their National Service. Their names were John Chamberlain and Brian James. At least we were company for each other on our journey into the unknown.

After arriving at Waterloo, we made our way to Kings Cross for the connection to Warrington in Lancashire. I suppose on reflection it was the sign of the times that ninety per cent of the passengers on the train to Warrington were young men reporting for National Service.

We were in a compartment for six people and the discussions were soon underway; it was as if we had known each other all of our lives. We all had a lot to say; our occupations, girlfriends, and what we were to expect in the RAF. Of course, what you expect and what you get is so different. Anyone who has had this experience will agree with what I say.

The discussion turned to discipline. In our group of six, one had rather more to say and I think was a lot more vocal than any of us. He was an Eastender and his hair was collar length. His comment was as follows, "No f . . . . corporal is going to tell me what to do, or to get my hair cut."

I happened to spend my twelve weeks' training, or square-bashing, with this person, and need I say he was told what to do and did it in a hurry like the rest of us, and so the f . . . . . . corporal always had his way, without question.

After what seemed like a short journey, the train pulled into Warrington station at about four o'clock, and we were very surprised to see a couple of RAF NCOs at the station. We were all herded together and directed to the station forecourt. We were pleased to see three or four RAF coaches waiting for us; we had fully expected to have to make our own way to RAF Padgate from the station. We were soon on our way. I had no idea of the distance from the station to the camp, but it didn't seem to take all that long.

AT PADGATE

My first sight of Padgate was the aircraft outside the main gate; I think it was a Spitfire. All of us were allocated billets and a corporal introduced himself. He wasn't a D.I., I think he was a general duties wallah. He couldn't have been a D.I. — he was too nice!!!

Twenty-two people were in our billet and we were to be together for the next three months. I will list here the various occupations that we had followed; two teachers, one atomic research worker (with a degree), a train driver, a postman, two cooks, carpenters, tool-makers and engineers. There was a complete mix, we were from all parts of the United Kingdom.

"Be ready in ten minutes and I'll take you to the cookhouse, we are right on tea time."

That suited all of us, we were so hungry. Considering the amount of people the cooks were catering for, I always considered the food quite reasonable. I will always remember my first meal in the RAF. Here it is; mashed potato, peas and black pudding; plenty of bread and butter; stewed apple and custard, and tea from the urn. Not knowing the ropes, we were a bit reluctant to go round for second teas. No notice was taken so we had what we wanted. Of course some were not so happy with the quality of the food; I can only think that they had been thoroughly spoiled by their mothers regarding food, and these rough and ready meals were not to their liking. I had never seen black pudding in my life, but I scoffed it just the same.

I failed to mention at the beginning of this phase that our first issue of equipment from the corporal was the good old "mug and irons" and if anything sticks in one's memory, it is of erks walking to and from the cookhouse carrying their mug, knife, fork and spoon and dipping them in the hot water tank after the meal which was usually outside of the building.

After tea, we could please ourselves what we did in the evening. With a lot of the new boys, I made my way to the NAAFI; it was a good meeting point. I liked to sit and chat and enjoy a glass of beer. I started talking to a man, a complete stranger, and we were discussing the merits of football teams and their players. I had a feeling that the man I was talking to came from the West Country; his dialect seemed to have a distinct New Forest burr. This should have given me a clue to who he was. We carried on talking about football and I even had the temerity to ask if he played football. What I did not know, until I was told later, the man I had been talking to was one of the Sillett brothers, and I had not recognised an England player!! National Service was like that, you were likely to meet just about anyone. More of that later.

Our first real day in the Air Force started with a talk from our corporal in charge. His job was to guide us all to various offices, stores, clinics, the tailor and the dreaded barbers. He would control two billets at a time; about forty men. I would like to say that he was a decent man. He was always cheerful and very patient, answering all our questions in our strange new world.

The clothing store, I thought, was very well organised in dealing with batches of forty at a time. You entered one end of the store with nothing and came out of the other end with your kitbag, stamped with your RAF number and a complete kit. I will not claim it all fitted, but we were all to visit the tailor. After alterations our uniforms were a pretty good fit.

Our shirt issue gave me a problem, as I had never in my life worn a shirt with a separate collar and this is what these shirts were. We did have collar studs issued, but I had to ask one of the teachers how to fit them on. We had nicknamed him 'The Professor'. He came from Scarborough and, who knows, he may read this; kind regards if he does.

We were all keen to get into our uniforms and wanted to look our best. Our hats, or berets, gave us the biggest laughs as you could just not get them to fit. We tried hot water, cold water, pulling and stretching and after about three days of trial and error they became reasonable to wear. I think that the trouble was we had the hats first and then the haircut, or hair blitz! We were all really scalped! We went through the barber's shop as if we were on a conveyor belt. There were no niceties like "Something for the weekend sir". We sat in the chair and we were out again in what seemed like two minutes, minus our hair!

Our first taste of drill was to be learning the pay parade procedure. There was not a lot to it and we did our best to get it right, if only for the corporal's sake. The pay was twenty-eight shillings per week. We were only paid one pound with a promise that it would be made up later. This went on for twelve weeks. I still don't know what they meant by later, I am sixty-four now and I am still waiting! Perhaps it went on officers' messing bills?

Whilst I am writing about pay, after serving about six months, we were invited to join a savings scheme. It would be stopped from your weekly pay and I agreed to have a shilling a week put into the savings account, and I have never heard of those savings. I have often wondered what happened to that one shilling per week. I did write to RAF records, but they were not interested in opening a "can of worms".

The week at Padgate was very busy; collecting our equipment, attending medicals, having eye tests and hearing tests. I think we were all very surprised how easily we fell into our routine, and, dare I say, I really enjoyed the complete change in my life. Mind you, the real world was yet to come!

As I have stated, we were having more medical tests, and on about the fourth day we were lining up for a hearing test. Out of our group of forty recruits only one failed, and this decided his future in the RAF. He would be discharged within the next two days. Of course the cry went up "You lucky sod" but the unusual chap actually wanted to stay in the RAF and did appeal at the decision to discharge him, but it made no difference whatsoever; he was given a rail warrant for the journey home.

Out of all the equipment we had drawn, we were unable to draw webbing. We did draw a webbing belt and buckle as the only item of that particular category. We were all given a deficiency chit to cover us for kit inspections. I carried this throughout my Service; it meant less kit to clean and carry, and I don't mind telling you that suited me just fine. That little piece of paper was my prized possession!!

It was time to discard our civilian clothing. Our corporal informed us that our civilian clothing had to be parcelled up by us and posted home. We all agreed that it was a very good idea. Each of us had one small wardrobe in our bed space and it just would not carry civvy clothes and our service equipment.

Tonight was to be our domestic evening better known as "bull night". Spit and polish was due to become a way of life for all of us. We all had spent money on boot polish, Duraglit, dusters and other items for cleaning. This we bought in the NAAFI. What with the odd fry-up and a packet of fags, plus two nights in Astra at sixpence a go, our money was just about seeing us through until next payday.

After having had our breakfast, we were looking forward to a fairly easy morning, when, out of the blue, we had the order to pack our kit in double quick time, which we did, and we were marched to a hangar and, after a short while, over a hundred personnel were assembled. The rumours, as to be expected, were flying from all angles. We were going to West Kirby, Bridgenorth, Catterick and one or two others. None of those in fact. We were to entrain for RAF Innsworth, 13 S.OF.R.T.

POSTED TO INNSWORTH

We were coached to Warrington station, complete with a packed lunch, relevant documents to carry with us, identity card, medical papers, some sort of pay form, and the good old webbing deficiency chit. My service number was 2515786, a number I wouldn't forget, as I feel sure any of you who have been through this experience would agree.

Well, here we all were, out in public for the first time in our uniforms, and I had the sneaking feeling, the time that we all felt quite chuffed!! We were soon on the train and ready to go. I was pleased to be moving on. There had been quite a panic to get us prepared for moving, so I had the feeling that Innsworth had been a sudden decision.

We had reached Crewe on our journey and now it was everybody out as we had to change trains for Gloucester. I didn't mind this at all, the sun had begun to shine and we had to line up in single file along the whole length of the platform, facing the track. We had been waiting for about twenty minutes when a train came into view. It slowed to make its way through the station, heading northwards. So what? Just another train. No, not quite. The whole train, about seven carriages, was filled with soldiers. It passed within about three yards of us erks all decked out in our brand-new uniforms and our brand-new lily-white kitbags and service numbers stamped in black, and you might say, with tongue in cheek, "still wet". Some observant squaddie had spotted us standing there like sitting ducks well before they had reached the station, and they were well prepared. We had to stand there whilst they enjoyed pelting us with apple cores, orange peel, crusts of bread, any sort of rubbish that they could lay their hands on!! — as well as catcalls, whistling, all sorts of gestures and comments such as "Get your numbers dry", "Spaceship head" and a few others not quite so pleasant. We just had to stand where we were and endure this situation. But I believe, to a man, that we enjoyed the occurrence, and we all agreed that we would have done the same had we been in their situation. Even our NCOs were laughing. Need I say more? Except that I think it made our day almost as much as it did the squaddies.

It was just as well that we had had that light-hearted and comical event, because on our arrival at Gloucester station we were in for a rude awakening! Once again on our arrival, transport would be waiting for us, not the luxury of coaches, but lorries. These would take us to number 13 S.OF.R.T., RAF Innsworth. Innsworth to Gloucester is not very far and in no time at all we were at the main gate and slowly making our way to the billet lines.

AT RAF INNSWORTH

"Come on you lot, move yourselves." That was our first introduction to our beloved corporal drill instructors (or D.I.s). Our kitbags were thrown from the lorries onto the grass verges; grass, which I admit, had been kept very well.

"Hurry up, collect your kitbags and keep off the grass" said the instructors.

"But the kitbags are on the grass, Corp" we replied.

"Don't answer back and stand to attention when you speak to me" was the reply.

I decided at that moment that logic was not in the make-up of a D.I. Twenty-two erks at a time were allotted to their billets. Our flight of one hundred men would be known as 29a. We each had a bed space, with a small wardrobe and bedside locker, and the lino had been polished like glass.

We were in the process of sorting our gear and stowing away when the order came to stand by your beds. We would hear that order many times during our training at Innsworth. We were due for a talk from the D.I. who was in charge of our billet and who occupied a small room away from all of us erks. The basis of our lecture was to do as you are told in double quick time, or else. Of course we had already gathered as much, just judging by the first half an hour of our arrival. It would be a very strict regime. He walked up and down the billet spelling out what was to be expected of us; we would come to attention when he entered the billet, always call him corporal, and he carried on to say "When I say jump, you jump." For some reason it seemed that he took a dislike to me. Maybe it was because I had had the audacity to walk on the grass. I just don't know, but that was how it would remain all through my training. I would like to stress here that I was never bullied, we just did not get on very well. I would also like to say that he would always be turned out smart and an example to us all. We had five D.I. corporals and their leader was a sergeant, all very well turned out, and overall they were a very decent bunch of NCOs.

It was soon tea time and I was very glad the time had come for my nosh. The meal we had was very palatable, and, again, there was plenty of bread and butter, jam, and as much tea as we wanted.

As well as square-bashing, Innsworth was also a school of cookery. The length of the course to learn cookery was sixteen weeks. A part of the cooks' training was to be let loose in the cookhouse on their twelfth week, and their culinary efforts would be tried out on us rookies. Some were good, some were bad and others really awful. The fact is we were being built up to such a peak of fitness, and our hunger was such that we would eat virtually anything served in front of us, but I hated lumpy mashed potato, and we had a lot of that. Very often I asked for second helpings, but not spuds, of course. I think that I would be right in saying that this particular cookhouse catered for at least five hundred men. One thing I did notice was that the permanent staff on the station were not to be found in the rookies' cookhouse; they had their own. I wonder why? We soon found out who the fussy eaters were out of our group of people!!

I had had an eventful day and by nine o'clock I was ready to hit the sack. I have often wondered how it was I could go to sleep so easily in an open type dormitory situation, and now that I am much older I must have complete silence before I nod off. I suppose not being able to sleep so well is one of the penalties of being old. I was not alone in wanting to go to sleep, just about everyone was crashing out, and the billet soon became very quiet.

I was awoken from a deep and wonderful sleep though in the morning, and it seemed as if all hell had been let loose. I had a rude awakening from our NCO whose turn it was to get us out of bed. He was making a terrible noise by banging on the metal lockers, and, at the same time, shouting "Wakey Wakey", and it did not do any good turning over for another five minutes; "OUT". You just had to get out. We were all complaining, not to the D.I., of course, but to each other. "It's only half-past bloody five" was the general cry.

First job — wash and shave; twenty-two men trying to share

eight washbasins. The last in the queue had to wash and shave in cold water as all the hot had been used.

One job that I hated, but one we all had to do, was folding our bedding. It had to be folded in a particular way and placed in at the foot of the bed, but it also had to be in line with the blankets and pillow on the next bed and so on. We also had to clean our bed space and make sure that our lockers were in apple-pie order. All this was before breakfast.

Breakfast was usually a very hurried affair, which was a pity because sometimes kippers were on the menu and I could have as many as I wanted, whereas if it was bacon and egg, I had to have what I was given. Not a lot of people like kippers!!

At Innsworth, the first week of training would be taken up with general duties, mixed with quite a lot of drill instruction. General duties entailed mainly labouring jobs, cleaning in the NAAFI or sergeants' mess; cutting grass, etc., and being a dogsbody to everyone. We all had to wear grey-green denims.

Every day one member of the billet had to be billet-orderly which meant that he had to be in the billet all day doing cleaning and making sure all was spick and span. Also I think it was for some reason of security.

A training programme would be made up of three-quarters of an hour periods which consisted of P.T. education and many subjects that the powers thought that we had need of. The venues for these activities were spread around the station and we either marched or had to double. This went on throughout the day. Most evenings were taken up with cleaning your kit and cleaning the billet. Not one person was allowed to walk on the floor; we all skated around on pieces of folded blanket. This avoided scratching from our studded boots, and at the same time polished the floor! Of course, NCOs did as they pleased.

We all had a pleasant surprise as few of us realised that we were coming up to a Bank Holiday, which meant that we would be allowed to travel home. Permanent staff had to have their Bank Holiday, including D.I.s, so very few people would be on the station. Who were we to argue?

The threat of stopping our passes was used time and time again if the D.I.s were not satisfied with our performance, especially in our drilling. I realise now, of course, that the threat of stopping our passes was a con trick, but we all believed them at the time.

In the short time that I had been training, my fitness had improved no end. My weight was only about nine and a half stone and I felt really on top of the world.

The Bank Holiday soon arrived and we were given our passes to fill in. These were signed by our flight officer; also we were issued with a ration card. I know that I speak for all of the flight, when I say the Bank Holiday break was something that we were looking forward to with a great deal of excitement; I would be arriving home in uniform for the first time and I would be eating home-cooked food and meeting up, once again, with a lot of my friends. I would also be dancing and enjoying myself at the South Parade Pier in Southsea, which, sad to say, is no longer with us as a dance hall, and has been replaced with those ghastly slot machines. It was really wonderful having some days at home, but always at the back of my mind was the thought of having to report back to Innsworth to continue training. That is how it had to be and the break seemed over in a flash and it was soon time to return.

In no time at all we were back in the routine, but by this time the senior NCO was about to introduce us to the .303 Lee Enfield rifle, mainly for drilling. Shooting and target practice would be a little later in our programme. Instruction was given by the "RAF Regiment". The Lee Enfield is a heavy rifle and very awkward to handle. I found it tricky, the reason being I have small hands and gripping the rifle was a problem. Shouldering arms gave me a sore shoulder in the initial stages of the drill, but like everything else and everyone else, I had to cope with it.

One thing that I did not suffer with was foot blisters caused through drilling and, of course, the dreaded ammunition boots. I had been wearing boots in my job in the building trade and for this reason wearing boots at this time caused me no problems, but my heart went out to those who had only ever worn shoes. They had very badly blistered feet.

Surprisingly, progress was being made in our drill. Out of a complete shambles came some form of order, which pleased our senior NCO. Having a programme of three-quarters of a hour periods was beneficial. We did have time to relax away from physical training and drilling.

Now it was time for a lecture by an officer on atomic warfare. Why atomic warfare I have often wondered, but I suppose that in 1951 it was relevant. We would double to the education block and almost every time we would have to wait for the officer to arrive. We didn't mind this as the May of 1951 was really kind to us; lots of glorious sunshine, and I can't recall it raining.

So there we were waiting for the lecturer, and maybe sometimes, he would be as much as thirty minutes late. It was quite easy to relax on a warm Spring day and during the lecture it was not unusual to nod off. The officer would realise that this was happening and he would pounce on anyone whom he thought was not paying attention.

As I have said, we were a very mixed bunch, trade-wise, and with us was a man who held a degree in energy and engineering, and this was the man that the officer chose to stand in front of the class and carry on the lecture. The officer was pretty sure that the man would make a fool of himself, and that would be his punishment for not paying attention. Not so! He knew more about atomic energy, and the subject that the officer was trying to impart to the class; and, into the bargain, his lecture was more interesting by far, and we remained awake. I would imagine that was a trap that very many officers and NCOs fell into, as I will enlarge upon.

Very often, whilst waiting for the arrival of an officer, the NCO in charge would point his finger at an individual and order him to stand and give the class brief details of himself and what his employment was before his call to National Service. This was always of interest to me and I am sure many others as it helped to pass the time and was always done in a light-hearted manner. However, in a flight preceding 29a, was a man who was employed as a footman to the royal family in London and he was singled out by the NCO to stand up and give an account of his occupation in civvy street.

He stood up and gave the briefest of details about his job, which were as follows: "I was a footman at Buckingham Palace . . . . ." and refused to say any more.

The NCO, not realising the situation he was in, insisted that he explain more about his job. This he would not do, and for an AC2 in training to refuse an order from a D.I. took a lot of courage. It became a major incident. But the AC2, who had friends in high places, came out the winner and the NCO was reprimanded.

What I have just written is not something that I heard through the camp grapevine. Later in my Service life, I was to work with this man as commanding officer's batman, and I heard the complete story from him. More of him and I later in the story. Once again it was a case of "careful where you tread" to officers and NCOs. The footman and I were to work together at RAF Hednesford, but I will not name him as I have no wish to embarrass him

At this stage I would like to explain a little about RAF uniform. NCOs and other ranks are very much the same, the working uniform and the dress uniform, or best blue. No indication of rank was worn by an AC1 or AC2. The working blue was a button-up tunic, also worn by officers and NCOs. Designation of rank would be a pale-blue quarter wide tape worn on his shoulder, just about visible. His cap badge would differ from other ranks.

I was walking through the camp one evening as the sun had begun to set and was very low in the sky, shining right into my eyes. Out of the glare, walking towards me, came another person. The big question was "Is it an officer, or an erk like me?" To salute, or not salute? I could not face the ridicule that I would receive if I saluted another erk. So we approached each other and I still could not see the other fellow properly, so I decided, very quickly, that I would not salute. My big mistake. He was an officer, and a pilot officer at that.
"Come here" he cried.
I turned, walked up to him, came to attention and saluted.
"Why did you walk by me without saluting?"
I just did not have a good reason, apart from the sun in my eyes, but he insisted on an explanation. So I came up with "I'm sorry Sir, but I thought you were just another recruit."
I think if I had been in the Navy he would have had me flogged with a cat-o'-nine-tails; the look on his face was one of disbelief. "You will walk up and down saluting me until I tell you to stop, now move!!" was his answer.
Well, this little snot of an officer made me do this for fifteen minutes until I had satisfied his inflated ego!

I don't know how it came about, but a good percentage of the flight became involved with evening football. The venue was an aircraft hangar and we played in plimsolls; shirts versus skins. We played hut against hut. NCOs played in their particular hut teams with no quarter asked nor given.

Playing football did not excuse us in any way from kit or billet cleaning; this had to be done before football. How we found the energy for all this I really do not know. Maybe the secret was that we were all so young and fit. However, this was one of the happier moments during training.

Now for a happening of a more serious nature. In recent months a lot of attention has been drawn to the matter of germ warfare. For example Porton Down, the Gulf and an area in Dorset, all denied, of course, by the MOD.

During the course of our training we all had many visits to the doctor. On one such visit we were all given an injection in our arm. I was never told the reason for, or the nature of, this injection and I never had the nerve to ask, after all I was a mere AC2. It was a case of "Do as you are told, or else."

A day or two after the injection, everyone was beginning to feel an irritation on both shoulder blades. The irritation continued until we had nice round scabs, roughly the size of a five-pence piece. These scabs had very very thick crusts on them. These scabs were checked on a regular basis, and mine stayed with me for about two weeks.

In the light of all the questions being asked about the MOD and germ warfare experiments, I am asking the question "Were I and many thousands of National Servicemen being used as guinea pigs without being told?" I think that this is a comment worth making. One more thing that I would like to add on this subject, is that the doctors did seem to be over-interested in the results of the injections. I will leave you to make your own conclusions.

As I stated earlier, it was the duty of the RAF Regiment to instruct us in weaponry. This included the Bren gun, the Lee Enfield and other small arms. I did enjoy firing the Bren gun. It was also the Regiment's job to take us through the assault course. We would have a couple of trial runs, and be marked or assessed on the final run. The final run would take place during the sixth week of our training.

The day arrived for our run, a very hot and sunny day and we were formed into groups of four. The group that I was in were to be the first group to run. It was not an easy course, but it did test an individual's fitness. As I have stated, we were all very fit. At the end of the run we were all soaked to the skin and very muddy. Being the first group to complete the run gave us the wonderful opportunity to return to our billets and have the first use of the showers and get cracking with the job of cleaning our equipment. After the excitement of the day I became very tired; the time was nearing nine o'clock and I was ready for bed, and in no time at all sleep was upon me . . . . . . "Oh no, not reveille, I don't believe it! Where did the night go?" That was not all, I just could not move my limbs without a hell of a struggle and I was sweating with some kind of fever.

My pal in the next bed, John Chamberlain, also from my home town of Portsmouth, helped me all he could. The NCO advised me to report sick. As I have said, I could hardly move my limbs, but such was the crazy world of the Services, I still had to fold my blankets, clean my bed space, pack my personal toiletries to take to the hospital. I thank goodness that John was there to give me a helping hand, but I still had to walk it to the hospital which was outside of the main camp, roughly a mile away.

I started to make my way to the main gate and guardroom. Perspiration was running down my face and into my eyes. Even at this time of day, 8 a.m., the roads of the camp were very busy with people making their way to their places of work. Everybody looked very much the same to me; civilians, NCOs, erks and officers. "Salute laddie" I was told a number of times, but I was oblivious to it all. Past the guardroom and across the road I would soon have been at the hospital, but no such luck, not yet anyway. I was called over. "Do you ever salute?" he bawled at me, and as any ex-serviceman would know, NCOs always had the habit of shouting at you nose to nose. I just could not answer. "Are you deaf as well as stupid?" he asked. Then it dawned on this individual that something was amiss. "Come into the guardroom. I think that there is something wrong with this man, Sarge" he said.

"I can see that. The poor bugger looks ill. Get him to the hospital" said an NCO with a bit of compassion. A provo at that.

He did me a big favour by having the corporal escort me to the hospital. He was able to take me into the doctor ahead of the others reporting sick.

By this time I was sweating profusely. I don't remember the doctor asking me anything, but I do remember being put to bed at once. It is a strange fact that once you have been used to having tidiness and routine drilled into you, you carry on with that routine, whatever the circumstances, and that is just what I did. I unpacked my small pack, stored the contents into a bedside locker and the clothes that I discarded were folded into a neat pile. I was feeling pretty ill at the time, but the routine of training still prevailed.

Once into bed, I began to drift into a long and glorious deep sleep. When I did finally awake I was told that I had been sleeping for thirty-six hours. A curious thing about my "big sleep" was this: I had been taking tablets every four hours, given to me by a nurse. Even stranger was the fact that I had been oblivious to all this going on.

"I have been waiting for you to wake up, Mick" said a voice.

It was after hearing my name that I took a proper look at the man standing by my bed. 'My God, it's Bob Taubman!' I thought. This man's father was a leader of the youth club in Portsmouth, and Bob was a man of my age that I had played football with in civvy street, and now he was my nurse. I had no idea that he was at Innsworth, or that he was a nurse. It was very nice to see a friendly face because I was still feeling a bit low. I think to say "It's a small world" is an understatement.

After the third day, I was making good progress. As much as anything I think it was the complete rest making me feel so much better. My biggest worry, and the cloud on the horizon, was the dread of being re-flighted. In the Service jargon of the time, this meant being put back into a more junior flight to make up for the lost time in training. For me this would have been a disaster. It would mean new NCOs, a hundred new faces and another four weeks' square-bashing. What erk would want that? Certainly not yours truly. It would be the decision of the senior NCO whether you would be put back a flight, or to be allowed to continue in your old flight upon discharge from hospital.

Well, friend, the decision went my way. I was told personally by the sergeant that I would stay in 29a. Why he made that decision I shall never know, but I was so pleased and relieved and very grateful. So, there you are, not all drill instructors were pigs.

I will never know why I had to be hospitalised, not the real reason. I did feel very groggy and the doctor suggested that it may have been twenty-four hour influenza. I still wonder about those secret injections. Could there have been a connection?

On my return, the first period of the day was a visit to the career's officer. I could never see the point of having a career's officer in the days of National Service. What you did in civilian life to earn a living, carried no weight at all. If the Air Force required you to do a particular job, then you were put into that job. However, we all had to go through the process.

My turn came for the interview. I had been looking through the list of jobs, and one or two caught my eye; particularly airfield construction. I had been working in the building trade since leaving school, so I thought that I had a good chance of being accepted for that particular job. I thought wrong. I would have to sign on for another four years to have any chance. That idea never appealed to me so I enquired about the job of parachute packer. It was the same situation as my first choice, I would have to sign on for more years. A batman/waiter's job was on offer. It would mean working in the officers' or sergeants' mess, and that is what I would become after training.

It was at this time that I decided to sign on for another year, mainly for the extra £1 per week. I intended to send ten shillings a week home to my mother, but being the mother that she was, she flatly refused to accept it.

I never had any regrets about taking that job as I made some very good friends. I am still in contact with two of them now after nearly fifty years. John Waddington from Chorley in Lancashire and Ron Dobbs from Caldicot in South Wales. I have good memories of those two scallywags.

Our training was well advanced by this time and we were all looking forward to the passing out parade, and, of course, the party afterwards. The parade went according to plan. It is very surprising what can be achieved in ten weeks; from being an absolute rabble when we started, we had become a presentable drill unit. This was a happy time for everyone. We had our new posting to look forward to and, best of all, a week's leave before proceeding to our new stations. Some of the luckier ones would be going abroad. Not all overseas postings were to be looked forward to, as some could be war zones.

Our 29a flight had been working very hard over the last ten weeks to reach the expected standard, and having a party in the NAAFI, was a good way to celebrate. The five NCOs joined us and this gave us the opportunity to have a chat with them, and we could all

29a Flight, D.I. Vincent, RAF Innsworth, 1951

see them as different people off parade.

It was out of bed early the next day, in spite of the party and a few hangovers, but everyone was in a good frame of mind. Today was the day that we would all hear of our new postings; everyone, that is, except me. The sergeant visited each billet to give us the good or the bad news, depending on the individual concerned. Very few, if any, were posted to the same RAF station, unlike the Army where freshly-trained units were normally kept together. For the Air Force it was new places and new faces. A great pity because some good friendships were formed during training. For me it was back to good old Innsworth.

POOL FLIGHT

Pool flight was the situation for any airman who had yet to be found a new posting. Pool flight billets contained about forty people at any one time and were situated next to the training billets. The NCOs in charge were not D.I.s and we were treated as permanent staff. Our task was permanent fatigues until a new posting was found. I was to spend three weeks in Pool flight and I did not mind it one bit.

We were required to muster at 8.30 a.m. outside of our billets in readiness for the two corporals to select men for various fatigue duties around the station, and I feel sure that we were the surplus of men that they had no idea what to do with! If you consider that the station was full of new recruits doing first week training fatigues, you will understand what I mean. Not that any of us cared a hoot. In Service lingo it was a good skive! If six of you were detailed to the sergeants' mess, probably two would skive off somewhere else.

My first assignment was with six others to go to the bathhouses to clean the baths, etc. Between the seven of us it amounted to about two hours' work, the rest of the day would be ours. The venue, more often than not, would be the NAAFI in the morning for an hour's tea break, and the same in the afternoon. There just was not work for so many people. The millions of hours wasted in this way during the period of National Service, I think, is best forgotten.

Pool flight was left very much alone, not quite out of sight, but very much out of mind. Very often I would watch the happenings of the new tenants of the ex-29a billets. These people, of course, would be just starting their training, and as I watched them drilling, etc., I began to realise what a difficult job it was for the D.I.s to get one hundred raw recruits up to the standard required for passing out in the period of ten to twelve weeks' training. Please believe me when I say that I am not gloating; our lot were just as much of a rabble to start with — we reached the required standard, but only through the excellent work of the D.I.s.

My days at Innsworth were coming to an end. My leaving time would be three days hence. I was to be posted to RAF Hednesford in Staffordshire. I had expected to be posted to RAF Spitlegate for trade training, but like all good airmen, I just did as I was told.

I had no regrets on leaving Innsworth. As good as the skive was, it had become a bit wearing in Pool flight. I decided that it would be a good idea to walk across to the training lines to say cheerio to the D.I.s who had hounded us for our own good. I did not believe it then but they were absolutely right! We shook hands and I made a point of saying thanks to the sergeant for allowing me to stay in 29a flight after my bout of illness. One of the corporals had been responsible for me being given four days' jankers, but that was all forgotten when we shook hands and wished each other good luck. I am sure that he would not be offended if I mentioned his name; it is Mr Vincent and I think that he came from Watford.

I have always considered the square-bashing days of my Service to be reasonably good. Some of you might say what a load of cobblers. All it was really was learning to accept discipline. No big deal really. If you were prepared to knuckle down and try your best you were sure to get through, and Service life would only get better after the initial training. I am talking peacetime, of course. I really admire the people who preceded me in the dark days of World War Two; an entirely different situation to my easy ride.

My time to leave Innsworth had arrived. I had my documents and railway warrant to proceed to Hednesford via Birmingham. They even gave me and my kitbag a lift into Gloucester station, and also a packed lunch. You might say that I had become an airman proper. I was to find out that my Service life would never be humdrum, even in peacetime.

My train ride to Birmingham was uneventful. I was to change trains for a connection to Hednesford, or at least that was the idea, but, in all my innocence, a train to Hednesford was but a dream. I was told that the nearest that I could get to my destination was a tiny halt called Brindley Heath. That sounded just fine but little did I know what awaited me on my arrival at Brindley Heath. Anyone reading this who was ever stationed at Hednesford would remember "Kitbag Hill". I have no idea of the real or proper name for this stretch of road that I had to negotiate before reaching the camp. From the halt to the camp was one long steep climb. Simple for a young, fit person, I agree, but I was carrying all of my kit, and into the bargain the temperature was in the seventies. It seemed like a never-ending slog. I stopped to rest many times, hoping that maybe some vehicle would happen by and offer a weary airman a lift. No such luck. I had to find out the hard way the meaning of the name "Kitbag Hill". The camp has closed now. I wonder if that hill has retained its name?

RAF HEDNESFORD

How many servicemen have ever been pleased to see a guardroom? I am not ashamed to admit that I was glad to see this one. When I told the S.P. that I had walked from the halt, he lost no time in telling his two colleagues and I think it made their day, even more so when they informed me that to obtain a lift to the camp all I had to do was telephone, and transport would have been provided. I suppose one has to live and learn, but what a greenhorn I was.

After the hilarity was over, it was down to business. After going through my papers, he had a discussion with his fellow S.P.s about my accommodation. Luckily for me transport billets were filled. These billets were for new arrivals and all stations had them. They were usually pretty crummy. I was given directions to a billet occupied by all members of the RAF Regiment. It seemed a bit odd; a mere AC2 occupying the same billet as corporals, some of whom had been sergeants and had been demoted for some reason or another.

I enjoyed the short time that I was billeted with these lads; a more down-to-earth group of people I have yet to meet. I will be honest and say that I was not very impressed with Hednesford. The accommodation was of the wooden hutment type. In fact I cannot remember seeing a brick building. The station was spread over a very large area and hardly any of it on level ground. It was situated in the heart of a coal mining area in Cannock Chase. Even parts of the main parade square had begun to sink, due to subsidence. However, the surrounding countryside was really lovely, a real treat for country walking.

My place of employment, the officers' mess, stood right on the edge of the station, about half a mile from my own billet; so it was not in a very good position for going on and off duty, especially in the inclement weather. I was to be billeted with the regiment for about three weeks, and I must say that they never seemed to mind having an AC2 in their midst. On the contrary, I became very useful to them.

Part of my work as a batman/waiter was taking care of the officers' uniforms which involved some ironing, putting a nice sharp crease in the right place. We were very well equipped for doing this work. In short, we had the right tools for the job. The Regiment lads were very aware of this and they were ready to take advantage.

"Pompey" (that was me) "will you do me a favour?"

"Sure, what it is?" I would reply.

"I would like you to press my best blue."

This was one of the corporals off to a dance in the evening. I did quite a lot of pressing for all of them. You bet your sweet life that I did. For every uniform I pressed I received a shilling; a nice little earner, you might say. A nice little supplement to my twenty-eight shillings a week. We had an understanding that if a best blue was hanging on my locker door, then it would be a silent request for a good press up! I obliged accordingly. This routine was to save me a lot of bother. I was in line for a 252 (charge), but for that routine of ours it would have been me on a fizzer. I will explain. A particular sergeant loved to do orderly sergeant, he enjoyed catching people out for really trivial reasons. In my job I was involved with shift work, 6 till 2, 2 till 10 etc. If my particular shift for the day was 2 till 10 p.m. it meant that I could enjoy a lie in, and, very often, I would take advantage of this situation. Very often an orderly sergeant would pay a visit to our billet and would take no notice of an erk having a lie in, understanding, no doubt, that shift work would be involved. But not "Piggy" Evans. I was in the end bed in a line of ten. My peace was shattered by a voice from the open door at the far end of the billet. "If you do not get out of that bed Corporal, I will have your guts for garters."

Out of bed I got. Piggy never came into the billet, he just continued on his way. 'Wait a minute' I thought, 'why had he called me Corporal?' I half turned, and there it was hanging on my locker door, a best blue waiting to be pressed, carrying the regiment sign, chevrons two bar, crossed rifles, even a row of ribbons. So old Piggy, for once in his life, had been caught out. All the lads in the billet were very pleased that I had got away with it thanks to a press job. I often wonder what Piggy's reaction would have been had he realised his mistake. I think that he would have hanged himself for letting a 252 get away. One thing that I am sure of, is that he would not have seen the humorous side of the situation. There was no humour in our Piggy!!

I think that all ex-servicemen would agree, that most stations at some time would have rumours doing the rounds, and a favourite expression at Hednesford would be "What's the buzz?" Well, this buzz was that a large percentage of personnel were to be moved to a new station — RAF Wharton.

TO RAF WHARTON AND BACK

But this "buzz" was true. The question was who would be the people to be posted? I was on orders to be prepared to move in one week's time. On the given day I was to be on parade with all my kit and ready to go at 5.30 a.m. I did have on my mind that this order for me to move was a mistake, bearing in mind that I had only just moved to Hednesford. I made enquiries on a visit to the orderly room.

"You are definitely down to go. Are you 2515786 AC1 Franckeiss?" The corporal was holding a list of people who were to be posted to RAF Wharton, and he showed me my name on the list.

I had had no time to get established at Hednesford and I was looking forward to moving on to pastures new. The thing about Service life is it never takes long to make friends, and I had made a number in the short time in my place of work. One of those I regard as a special friend was a lad from Blackburn. We got on very well from the beginning of our friendship. His name, John Waddington.

The evening before departure, a big percentage of those leaving were in the NAAFI having farewell drinks and I was one of that number. Time to move was here, and, once again, a packet of sandwiches for everyone and transportation to the railway station. It sounds easy, doesn't it? Somebody had made a cock-up with the train times and we had to wait for three hours, but my troubles had only just begun.

On our arrival at Wharton we were all given temporary accommodation, and, surprisingly enough, a meal had been laid on.

Next day began the sort out; all trades to report to their respective places of work, after which you would be given a permanent billet.

"I am sorry, I have no details of you being posted here" said the mess sergeant, giving me the good news. Enquiries were made on my behalf, and the outcome? A trip back to Hednesford.

HEDNESFORD AGAIN

I feel sure than any ex-serviceman reading this will be doing so with a wry grin on his face, and I hear you saying "Nothing changes". I had to make my own way back to my old station and this time I requested and received transport from my arrival point back to camp.

I was not the only one on a wasted journey to Wharton. I was never told the reason for my excursion, but who would bother with just another erk? My billet this time was to be with my workmates, so I was back among friends, and into the routine of working once more. The officers' quarters were individual rooms, a standard service hut about twelve rooms, and the billets would be adjacent to, or very near, the main mess. In this instance the buildings were of wooden construction. Civilians were employed in a mixture of positions around the camp, and I had the pleasure of working with one of these people. He and I had the job of looking after twelve officers and their rooms. As I have already written, Hednesford was the centre of a mining area. Jim, my civvy partner, was an ex-miner. We worked together very well; the more I got to know Jim, the more respect I had for the mining community. Many a Saturday evening I would spend in Chasetown Working Men's Club with Jim and his family. If I was short of money, and very often I was, the invitation still stood "Come over, and have a drink, you don't need money." A very genuine man.

I will just dwell on the subject of drinking for a while. A meeting point for many of the lads was the Anglessey Arms in Hednesford. My memory fails me regarding the particular brew, but it was a very popular venue. Another reason, apart from the beer, was that it was a good area for crumpet hunting and maybe there was the root of the problem. We began to have at that particular pub many arguments, and more often than not, a woman would be involved.

Working in the area were miners imported from Italy and Poland. At this time there was a shortage of skilled miners in this country, and they were helping to fill the gap. It seemed to me that they were a very quick-tempered lot, and the use of a knife would be their way of settling an argument. The Military Police were called on many occasions to sort out the troubles and the end result was that the Anglessey Arms was deemed out-of-bounds to all RAF personnel. Even so we would still pop in for a sneaky pint now and then, after all, it was "crumpet country".

Any of you who were ever stationed at Hednesford, will remember the caravan outside of the main gate, otherwise known as the chuck wagon. A man and wife team were the proprietors of this enterprise, and a very good service they provided. Tea, coffee, hot dogs, sandwiches, crisps, chocolate, and it was not unusual for them to be sold out of everything on a summer's evening. It was a pleasure just standing there having a chat over a cup of tea and a hot dog.

Once again, it seems that it is the simple things in life that give so much pleasure.

RAF Hednesford — Left to right: Joe Bradbury, Manchester; R. Vickers, Middlesbrough; L. Syner, Birmingham

HITCHHIKING

How many of you ex-servicemen reading this story will have hitchhiked to make their way home? A good many I would say. It was just not possible to be able to afford the rail fare to go home on leave. On almost every occasion I hitchhiked. The distance never mattered to me. I would set off travelling light, always on my own, my shaving gear tucked into my top pocket and maybe my greatcoat, depending on the time of year.

Allow me to remind you of the date of these happenings — 1951-1954, well before the advent of motorways. Drivers of that period were very generous toward men in uniform and it would be very unusual for me not to succeed in getting home by hitchhiking. I really enjoyed the challenge and I firmly believe that a good many drivers liked to have someone to chat to. It was not very often that I would be making my way home at night, a 48-hour pass would be from 12 noon, normally for me on a Friday, but this time I was able to skive off on the Thursday night.

I was making very good time, until north of Banbury. The rain came pouring down and I was caught out in the open and walking up hill. The time was 11 p.m. approximately. It was not long before my greatcoat was heavy with water. Believe me, when I say that this is not a happy time for hitchhikers, but good fortune was to smile on me once more in the shape of a lorry climbing the hill. He slowed and stopped.

"You must be bloody soaking, jump in" said a voice.

I needed no second bidding; yet another kind lorry driver.

"Where are you heading?" he asked.

"Pompey" I replied.

"That is good, you can help me find Hamble, I have two Rolls engines for a factory near there" he said.

I was more than pleased to be able to direct him. The make of the lorry I don't know, but the engine was inside the cab under a cowling and, of course, the cab was very warm, sheer luxury.

"Put your gear over the engine, it will soon dry" he said.

It dried in no time at all. I travelled with this man as far as Fareham. We shook hands and I thanked him, but thank you seemed hardly enough.

I looked at my watch. It was 1.30 a.m. and I began my walk towards Portsmouth and almost at once a car stopped. I opened the passenger door and I was not a little surprised to see that it was a woman driver and she was all alone. What faith and trust everyone had in each other fifty years ago.

"Where are you going young man?" she asked.

"Portsmouth" I replied.

"I can help you, in you get" she said.

This kind woman took me to within a half a mile of my home in Milton Road. Once more I was truly thankful. I had no need to wake my parents, our front door was never locked. It was good to be home again and I lost no time in taking to my bed.

My journeys back to camp were always more conventional; 9.25 p.m. train to London and on from there. I had to be sure of getting back to camp on time and many thanks to my good old dad, who would always give me a quid to help me on my way. Always a gentleman.

As I have said, I hitchhiked many many times. I will continue relating some of the happenings and there are plenty of them. I promise that I will not bore you, but I will select just a few of the events that may interest or amuse you.

On another occasion I travelled overnight and I was lucky enough to pick up a ride from Castle Bromwich to London in a furniture van. It was midnight, very cosy, chatting to the driver, making our way through the night to London. He said that he made his usual stop at an all-night café for something to eat, and afterwards a short sleep in his cab. Did I wish to do the same? Why not? We would still make London in good time.

This was the plan and it is just what we did. The driver was asleep in seconds. I wanted to sleep, but this man's snoring drove me to distraction. It was the most awful noise I have ever heard. I suppose we stayed in the cab for about an hour, but to me it seemed like an eternity. Under my breath I was pleading with him to wake up. I wanted to leave the cab and continue on my way once more but two things prevented me from doing this; I had no wish to hurt the man's feelings, and I did not want to be the one to disturb him by opening the cab door.

He awoke and seemed quite cheerful. "That's better, did you sleep OK?" he said.

"Yes" I replied.

"Let us get to London" he said, and once more we were on our way.

I offered up a prayer of thanks. What right have I to criticise a hard-working man having forty winks?

Hitchhiking from RAF Debden in the east would mean that very often you would be given a lift by an American serviceman. The US Air Force had a number of bases in England at this time. They were a very friendly lot and usually it would be a weekend in London that they would be heading for.

Debden, I think that I am right in saying, is approximately forty miles from London, and was a very good start for my journey home.

I enjoyed a cigarette at this time in my life and I can recall a number of occasions when I was given cigarettes by these kindly Yanks.

I think that I have written enough on the subject of hitchhiking. I must have travelled many hundreds of miles by this method during my Service time. I often listened to stories told by servicemen on their return to camp. Usually the story would be of being picked up by a very attractive woman, and she would be driving a top of the range car, and would be in need of company for the weekend. An AC1 would be just the ticket. Well, it never happened to me. I think these lads just tried to live out their fantasies. These was always one who wanted to feed everyone the same old line. I have been a journeyman decorator for fifty years and never yet have I ever been propositioned, but I still hear the same stories from men in the trade. They, too, it seems, want to live out their fantasies. I hear you asking "Are you complaining?" Of course I am!

BREAK-IN

As I have mentioned, the officers' mess at Hednesford was isolated from the main part of the camp. It includes kitchens, dining hall, billiard room, lounge and general office; all of which became unoccupied by 11 p.m. This situation is ready-made for anyone intent on burglary, and, sure enough, it did happen.

The president of the mess and his committee decided that it would be a good idea for two members of staff to do a guard duty throughout the night. This is not as bad as it sounds. A room was to be allocated with two beds and the guards would be allowed to sleep one at a time. An emergency telephone number to the main guardroom was also put in place. Being armed was out of the question. By armed I mean any form of firing weapon. For our protection we had pickaxe handles, quite useful in its own way, and I must admit that having that to hand gave me a lot of confidence.

Our first tour of duty was uneventful and we began taking it for granted that nothing would ever happen. How wrong we were. I was in slumberland and I know my fellow AC1 was keeping silent watch.

"Wake up Pompey, I think I can hear something or somebody from the main door area" I heard.

I only needed to put my jacket on. We had agreed on commencement of this duty that we would sleep with the majority of our clothes on. Pickaxe handles at the ready, we made our way silently along the corridor towards the main door. If they were burglars they never had much regard for silence. The time was 1 a.m. We carried one torch between us. It is ironic that of all the billions spent on National Service, we were only allowed one torch; we were told that the batteries were too expensive!

"I think we need to call the guardroom" said Tom.

"OK you do that and I'll . . . . . ." that is as far as my talking went. An almighty crash was heard and the door was forced open. We both went forward with pickaxe handles raised and ready. I saw this person in the doorway and I struck the intruder on the shoulder. It was a bad shot. I did mean it for his head.

"You bastard. What do you think you're doing?" said a slurred voice.

I had a feeling that I had heard this voice before.

"I'll have you before the commanding officer for this. I am Squadron Leader 'So-and-So', and I want your bloody name and number" said the officer.

The other officer with him was the same rank. I knew them both, they had both recently gained their promotion and it was all too obvious by this time that they had been out celebrating their new rank, and were both very drunk.

"I command you to open the bar" said one.

This was the reason for the break-in, they wanted more drink. We didn't have the keys to the bar and said as much.

"If you don't open the f . . . . . . bar I will break the door down" one of them said.

By this time I had had as much as I could stand and I ordered them from the mess, also telling them that we were about to inform the guardroom.

"You do that and I'll make both of your lives bloody hell" was the reply.

I just did not care any more and I was convinced that we were in the right. "If you two don't piss off you will get this pickaxe handle over your heads" I told them.

Complete silence. Somehow I had got through to them. Two S.P.s were on the scene within five minutes of our telephone call. These two bloody officers had the audacity to order the police to put us on a charge. This didn't happen, but we were in front of the C.O. first thing in the morning explaining the events and giving the full story word for word. Whatever the outcome I was determined to stick to my guns.

After the interview we were told to wait until called. The two officers concerned and the two S.P.s were meeting the C.O. Out they all came and it was our turn again.

"I have considered very carefully the situation that you were both in, and I am prepared to forget that this horrible situation ever arose. I have had a long talk with the officers concerned and they have agreed to pay for the repairs to the mess door" was his verdict.

So, that was it, no action against us and no apology from the two officers. How could there be? I am sure you have noticed, also, no action regarding the officers. Can you imagine the charges and the outcome if two erks, or the like, had broken into the officers' mess?

A POSH FRIEND

It was after these events that I was appointed the commanding officer's batman. My partner in this job was the man that I had heard so much about during my training at Innsworth. His name, Patrick Taylor, and his civilian job was as a footman to the royal family in London.

We got along very well and I enjoyed working with him. We were in shift together when King George VI died in February 1952. It was a very bleak day and I seem to remember that it was snowing, as we stood together talking and looking out of the window. He had a lot of nice things to say about the king and he was very distraught on hearing of his death. In fact, I did see a tear or two on Pat's cheek.

I would just like to say a word or two about friends in high places. In November of 1951, Hednesford was to be visited by the AOC, which many of you know meant that all leave for all ranks would be cancelled for a period of time leading up to the AOC inspection. So the standing order of the moment would be "spruce up camp" or to put it into erks' terms "bullshit baffles brains!"

On reading the order regarding the cancelling of leave, it sprang to my mind that Pat Taylor had been telling me that he had been invited, and was looking forward to, the 'Royal Household's Staff Christmas Ball'.

"It looks as if you will have to miss out on the invite" I remarked. We were chatting over a cup of tea.

But Pat was not a bit perturbed. "You don't really think that I will not be attending, do you Mick?" was his response. "A letter is on its way to the right quarter, and this situation regarding my leave will be sorted out before you can say Jack Robinson" he added.

And how right he was. Within days the problem no longer existed. His leave had been granted. Pat was not a man to gloat, but he was all smiles when he told me the news. The group captain, our commanding officer, had given him the OK personally. Even that speaks volumes. A group captain would not normally say a word to an erk. Any sort of message would be passed on through a lower rank. Do you think that it had anything to do with the fact that at that time the king's equerry was Group Captain Townsend? As I have said, friends in high places!

Pat's home was in Tonypandy, and one of the newspapers in that area had a picture on the front page of Pat dancing with the Queen Mother and the heading read: "The only AC2 to dance with the Queen."

He was very proud of that picture, and I wouldn't mind betting that he still is.

BRASS MONKEYS

I have always said that Cannock Chase, the location of RAF Hednesford, is a very nice part of England, but the camp was situated more or less over the crest of a hill, with the wooden hutments facing north to south; which, in turn, is not very nice for keeping your billet warm.

There was an inner and outer door at each end. Unfortunately the doors were mainly ill-fitting, with at least an inch gap at the bottom and snow would find its way into the billets. The billets were built on brick piers, two feet off the ground, therefore forming a wonderful wind tunnel, and this method of building resulted in the floor being always cold to the touch. "Heating" if you pardon the term, was almost non-existent. Two stoves would be standard for these buildings, placed at third intervals in the billet to heat an area in the region of 60 x 20 feet. These would be coke-burning stoves and they were very tricky to keep going and provide a decent and even temperature. Each billet had a fixed ration of coke and almost always the ration was never enough. It would only be issued when the temperature was deemed to be low enough, and whoever the decision-maker was, he never seemed to get it right. We tried every way we could to get more coke, even resorting to raiding the coke compound, but that was soon stopped when guards were ordered to patrol the area. It was hard to come to terms with the fact that here we were smack in the middle of a Staffordshire mining area and we had to be rationed with winter fuel.

The other drawback, apart from the heating of our billets, was that the shortage of fuel curtailed our hot water down to a minimum. If a wash and shave was required in the morning with hot water, then six o'clock was the latest that you had to be in the ablutions!

A hot bath was out of the question.

The officers' mess had its own boiler house and with a permanent boiler man, so the result of this would be constant hot water for the officers use. What else?

A bonus for the staff was to sneak a bath now and then, but if you were caught perpetrating this deadly sin, and reported, it would mean being put on a fizzer (charge). And well, well, you have guessed it, it happened to me. Of course, if you don't get on with the senior mess steward, in this case a Sergeant Bloodworth, then you were in deeper trouble.

ME AND THE SARGE, AND JANKERS

Can any of you ex-servicemen imagine getting four days' jankers for taking a bath? I often wondered why I seemed to get up his nose. I did my best to steer clear of him, and a few of my fellow workers did likewise!

I never considered doing jankers any sort of problem. It meant reporting to the guardroom morning and evening and being inspected by the orderly officer, and also making sure that your boots and brasses were polished and that you had sharp creases where they should be in your uniform.

We were very lucky in the job that we were in, in that the officers were generally known to us, and us to them, and we tended to pass muster quite easily. I haven't mentioned that RAF Hednesford was also a training camp, and that being the case, the poor old square-bashers were on jankers for all sorts of trivial reasons and always a good number would be reporting to the guardroom. They would really go through the mill when it came to the inspection. Added to this would be 'fatigues', a couple of hours doing odd jobs anywhere on the camp; very often in the cookhouse, in the dreaded wash-up doing your best trying to get baked-on grease removed from the cooking tins with very limited cleaning gear. At least if the right corporal was on shift, a bit of extra grub was very likely to come your way, plus plenty of tea; so, as you can see, jankers was not all bad!

NO MEAN FEAT

Cleanliness is of the utmost importance when people are living in close proximity, but some things just cannot be helped; such as smelly feet. I do not know the medical or technical name for this condition, but let us just say that this poor lad's feet sent off a horrible odour. Not his fault in any way; he did just about everything that he could to try and solve the problem; he just had to live with it, and so did his fellow airmen.

The reason that I am writing about these particular feet, is to relate an odd and amusing episode at a dining-in night. A dining-in night is a night in which all officers are expected to attend or have a very good reason not to. In short, it was almost classed as a parade for officers. The dining room floor, being a raised floor, tended to give off a hollow sound when many waiters were walking very quickly between servery and dining tables. Also the floor was wooden. Unlike other airmen, who were issued with two pairs of boots, batmen/waiters had shoes and boots. Shoes were always worn on duty, but the officers complained that they were too noisy and the order came that we were to wear plimsolls whilst waiting at the table.

"But Sarge, if I do that my feet will smell to high heaven. Shoes are bad enough, so can I be excused plimsolls? My feet sweat like hell in those things" said the lad with the foot odour problem. He was almost begging the sergeant to save him from a great deal of embarrassment.

But no, the NCO, being the type of person that he was, dismissed the request, "You will do as you are told."

So, that was it. Plimsolls must be worn.

The dinner got under way and in full swing. Just let me put you in the picture regarding officers' meals. Any ex-serviceman reading this will know that officers' meals would mean a good deal more than a mug and irons job. Dinner and lunch; soup, roast, sweet, cheese and biscuits, coffee. Generally sandwiches and tea at four o'clock in the afternoon, and always a cooked breakfast. The kitchen had a civilian chef in charge of two civilian cooks and three RAF cooks. The food was always superb. But, as always, somebody would complain. The mess had a complaints' book and, almost without fail, every week some officer would find something to gripe about when it came to the food, when, in fact, there was nothing to complain about. I often wondered what these complaining officers thought when inspecting other ranks' messes where there was good reason to complain.

As well as living-in officers, there would always be living-out officers who would require a meal in the mess; usually a lunch. For this meal a casual meal record book would be kept in the dining room. The idea was for the officer attending for a casual meal to report his presence to a waiter, who would take his name to enter into the book. Some officers, it seemed, did not agree with the idea of paying for casual meals, and did their best to avoid paying by not having his name entered in the book. At this time, 1953, a lunch would have cost about one shilling and sixpence and a damn good meal at that.

Back to little Geordie and his problem feet. As the dining-in night progressed, the dining room became very warm, which is not really surprising; there would have been about one hundred officers attending this night. Between courses we would stand in the dining room at various points and we began to notice officers making faces at each other and very likely asking the question "Can you smell anything?" It was no coincidence. Little Geordie, he with smelly feet, would be the one nearest to the complaining officers. It was the combination of plimsolls, naturally smelly feet, and the heat of the dining room, which was making a cocktail of a really pungent odour.

Needless to say, we never gave the game away. In fact I think that the waiting staff rather enjoyed the evening. It was a case of old Bloodworth, in his usual way, disregarding common sense and reasonable requests.

SPORT AND SOUR GRAPES

The sporting side of life in the RAF was the plus side of doing your National Service. Of the thirty or so batmen/waiters in our section, twenty were involved in one form of sport, indoor and outdoor. I think it safe to say that football was our main interest. We had a good mix of Scots, Geordies and people from further south. We were able to put together an eleven that were a really capable side. Every opportunity that we had we would be training, a lot of the time with the football. A good competition at Hednesford was the Inter Department Cup competition, and to say that it was keenly contested would be the understatement of the year — no quarter asked nor given. We had played many games other than cup games and we more than held our own. I think it fair to say that our main opponents were a combination of two sections on the station; the police and the P.T. staff.

For some reason the S.P.s and P.T.I.s imagined that the officers' mess staff were a lot of pansies and would be a pushover. We had won two out of two against them and they were a little shell-shocked. The officer in charge of the two sections was a flight lieutenant and he could not bear the thought of mere waiters having a good football team. We had won our way through to the Inter Section Cup Final, and our old enemies, the S.P.s and P.T.I.s had also reached the final. For some reason we were ordered not to use the pitch for practise. The order came from the flight lieutenant in charge of the S.P.s and P.T.I.s. The pitch was in perfect order, and a little practise by us would have done no harm to the pitch whatsoever.

As silly as he order was, we had to accept it. Our skipper asked permission to use an aircraft hangar for an hour in the evenings.

We were told by the flight lieutenant that this would not be possible. At first we were very surprised, but considering this man's attitude towards us in the past, we put it down to bad sportsmanship, and he badly wanted his section to win the cup.

However, half the members of the team decided enough was enough, and went out onto the pitch with a football for a short practise session. A very big mistake. They were unlucky enough to be seen by the miserable officer and were all put on a fizzer. The result being that they were barred from playing in the final. In one foul stroke we had lost six players, mainly defenders. The replacements that we had were not of the calibre of the barred players.

On the day of the final, the team played their hardest, but we lost the cup. We were convinced that the 'officer and a gentleman' made sure that, come what may, his section would win the cup. We were all very unhappy, but that man had a very hollow victory. Some officers are good, and some are not so good.

A party had been planned, win or lose, and after all the disappointment we had a wonderful time, even though the beer in the NAAFI was the usual brew. That is to say, warm and headless.

CRANWELL

My name came up on orders. LAC Franckeiss to be posted on attachment to RAF Cranwell. I was quite pleased, it would be a welcome change, and of course, I had no idea at all what my duties would be. My orders were to report to RAF Cranwell in one week's time on the 2nd August 1952. A lot of the lads called me a lucky sod and wished that they could come too.

I collected my railway warrant and orders from the orderly room, then started my journey. I had to use the route planned by the orderly room. Did I say planned? From Hednesford to Birmingham, to Tamworth; all this to go north to Nottingham. At Tamworth I had an hour to kill waiting for the connection, and I entered in conversation with another LAC going to Cranwell on attachment; very likely for the same reason as myself, and sure enough it was.

By this time I was down to my last two shillings and feeling more than a little hungry, so we decided to look for the NAAFI or 'Sally Army'. I smoked at this time, as did my new-found companion, and we were both out of cigarettes. As luck would have it, a Salvation Army Hall was not too far from the station; so we were in luck. It was about midday and a meal was being offered for about sixpence; but, as I have said, money was short, and as well as something to eat we were hoping to buy cigarettes. We just asked for two teas, nothing to eat. The lady behind the counter looked at us in a manner that suggested that she was a little hurt. She asked us why we didn't want anything to eat and I explained to her that we were short of money, and what we did have was to be spent on cigarettes.

"How far have you got to travel?" she asked. Before we had chance to answer, she ordered us to sit down. "Now then, don't move, I will bring your meals" she said.

An order to be obeyed and a meal to be enjoyed. Cottage pie followed by rice pudding. We had the effrontery to ask about payment, but she would not hear of it; she was just glad to provide us with something to eat. That was the kind lady's last word on the matter.

I have written about this little interlude to try and even the score a little regarding the Salvation Army. Their work has often been scoffed at without good cause, but I have found them always willing to help, and their presence on any RAF station was always an asset.

We reported to Cranwell guardroom at about 5 p.m., and surprise, surprise, they hadn't received a signal about us, that was a greeting from the S.P. What is it about the Services and communications? "What are you here for?" he asked.

Of course, we had no idea at all, and so, in his eyes, we were the idiots. He directed us to the transit billet and told us to report to the officers' mess, sergeant in charge of batmen/waiters. That, at least, made sense, as we were both batmen/waiters.

It made a nice change as the sergeant was actually pleasant to us, but us being there was nothing to do with their mess. "Come back in an hour and get something to eat."

An offer we never refused, after all, it was sure to be better than the airmen's mess food.

The guardroom were still unable to tell us why we were at Cranwell, but assured us that they would know by the end of the day. At least they got that bit right. About twenty other personnel had been sent on attachment to set up a canvas summer camp for grammar school students, who were RAF cadets, and their teachers were RAF officers supervising.

We were all trades; cooks, batmen, drivers, drill instructors and a sergeant in charge. We all shared the work. The camp was to be set up on the field adjacent to the sports stadium. The teachers/officers never roughed it under canvas, they had cosy single rooms in wooden hutments with batmen/waiters supplied. So the two of us had the job of looking after the officers and helping to build the camp.

It was an easy number. The officers were away from their billets from eight in the morning, and the officers' mess had a cosy bar that they could spend the evenings in if they so wished. And not for them the field cooking; they were allowed to eat in the station officers' mess; and wonderful grub it was! We had a lot of meals in the batmen/waiters' staff room, only semi-official, of course.

The team's job was to set up camp before the cadets arrived for their summer break and everything had to be in readiness. Fortunately the weather proved to be a bonus; brilliant sunshine every day and the work was fairly easy. We were all looking forward to a 48-hour pass for the weekend.

Late on the Wednesday evening, a huge pile of straw was delivered to the site for filling the palliasse pillows and mattresses.

IS A 48-HOUR PASS WORTH A BOLLOCKING?

On Thursday, we tried our luck with a proposition to the NCO in charge. We asked if we could work on in the early evening filling the palliasses, and then leave early Friday morning for weekend off. He was a bit reluctant to agree, but as we were a separate unit from the main camp he said it would be OK. We were well pleased and set to with a will. As I have said, the weather was really glorious and shirt-sleeve order was the dress. Maybe some of you have had the task of filling palliasses, but for those who never have, I will tell you, you end up the day looking like a sweep. "What, with nice clean straw?" I hear you say. The dust and grime that is emitted from bails of straw is really surprising.

Come seven o'clock, and the task was completed. Thank God for that, now for a bath. We had a choice; the long way round to the bath block or a shorter route through the officer cadet lines. To train to be an officer aircrew at Cranwell, you had to be prepared to tolerate a really rigid course of training. Spit and polish was part of it and this part was carried out to the letter. We decided on a walk through their lines, but what we didn't know was that the night was domestic night, or bull night, and with that went a pre-inspection prior to the morning. Wing commander, flying officer, sergeant, corporal, billet orderly, this was roughly the format for walking through and inspecting every billet, through one end and out the other. It was just our luck for the two of us to be walking past the entrance to one of the billets as the group came out.

"Stand where you are" we heard.

As I have said, we looked like a couple of tramps.

"Who the bloody hell are you two specimens?"

There we stood with the five of them looking at us as if we were some kind of aliens; after the biggest bollocking of my life and a warning that if ever one of us was even seen near these lines again all sorts of things would happen to us, and, I believe, shooting was one of them.

I thought that we had a fairly good reason for looking like we did and I think the wing commander realised this, after we had explained the situation. Perhaps the reason for the officer's concern was justified, after all he did not want the officer cadets to see the real world, did he?

A good rollocking is all part of Service life, and that is all we had, and we both knew that it could have been worse.

True to his word, the sergeant let us skive off early on the Friday morning; my pal off to his home in Middlesborough, and me hitchhiking my way home to Pompey.

Me with good friends still in civvy street

SKEGGY

I enjoyed my attachment to Cranwell, and my time there coincided with the August Bank Holiday (or grant). We were entitled to this as a matter of course, so the two of us decided on a weekend in Skegness, which, I think, is about forty to fifty miles from Cranwell. Hitchhiking, we decided, was the way to get there.

Luck soon came our way in the shape of an old coach which had been hired by a group of men going on a fishing trip, and a happy bunch they were too. A bit of a problem that we had, was trying to understand their dialect. I just hoped that I said yes and no in the right places.

Skegness was really teeming with people, all there to enjoy the August Bank Holiday. We managed to get a bed each at the YMCA.

We were really enjoying ourselves at Skeggy and we were to go to a dance in the evening. It was at this dance that we became attached to two young ladies and we really thought that our luck was in when they told us that they were staying in a caravan just outside Skegness. The dance finished at midnight, and being the gallants that we were, we asked to walk the two ladies home. What they didn't tell us was that the caravan was at Seaview, a very long walk from Skegness, but I think that we both had visions of not having to walk back that night. How wrong we were!!

After what seemed like walking fifty miles, the caravan site came into view, but strange to say, the lights were on, but even more strange was that one of the ladies knocked on the door.

"I wonder if Aunty's back yet?" she said.

Aunty was in and the girls introduced us.

"Do come in, and have a cup of cocoa before you walk back" she said.

So there you are, 'Win some, lose some'.

In due course we started our way back to Skegness, two very tired airmen who had just learned a lesson to never take things for granted.

Walking back had rather a humorous moment. Of course, it was pitch-black and we were in open country and there was no vehicle of any sort in sight. Lincolnshire is a very flat county with very deep drainage ditches either side of the country roads. Being the gentleman that I am, I walked to the edge of the road to relieve myself (all that cocoa, no doubt) and straight into the ditch I tumbled. But glory be, it was dry. No damage was done and we laughed our way back to the YMCA, tired, but happy, and with a tale to tell the lads back at Cranwell.

My stint at Cranwell was due to come to an end. We were in the process of dismantling the camp, and I was ordered to report to the orderly room to hear the words "You are to report back to RAF Hednesford."

That was a surprise! Our earlier orders were to leave on a later date. My attachment to Cranwell had been for eight weeks, and I look on my time there as one of the better periods of RAF life.

Flying training at Cranwell was an ongoing event and it was possible for erks to request a flight, and it was granted at the discretion of the officer in charge. I reported to the flight office and was offered a flight in a "Prentice". I had to draw a parachute and in that little craft you were seated next to the pilot on top of your parachute.

We were soon in the air, taking off from a grass track. This was my first flight. I had a wonderful view of Lincoln Cathedral from the air, and spectacular views of the East Coast, so I can safely say that I have flown in one of the smallest aircraft and one of the biggest, a Jumbo 747. That is my claim to fame. I did fly in a Lincoln and also a Dakota and, I suppose, for an RAF National Serviceman to be able to say that I did actually fly, is a bit unusual in itself.

HEDNESFORD AND PORTON DOWN

So, it was back to Hednesford, this time, I am happy to say, by a quicker and more direct route. Someone with a brain in the orderly room?

During my return journey, I had the privilege of a packed lunch and very good it was to eat. I was informed at Cranwell that it was standing orders for an official traveller to be issued with a packed meal. Better late than never, I suppose.

I was a bit apprehensive as to the reason for my sudden recall to Hednesford. At this time, 1951-1954, there were a lot of conflicts going on in the world; namely Malaya, Kenya, Korea, Aden and Cyprus, and I will say here and now that I had no wish to be involved. Some of you will probably call me a coward, but just remember Dear Readers, like thousands of others, I did not ask to join the Service, and I don't suppose that many of those men killed in those wars did either. In more recent times the Falklands War in 1982 was, in my opinion, a war to save certain politicians' political skins, the result of which was 250 deaths and many injured; and, of course, many young Argentinians lost their lives for the same reason.

I arrived back at Hednesford via Brindley Heath halt, and I had that wonderful experience of the walk to camp, which included "Kitbag Hill". As luck would have it, I was just in time for tea. It was whilst having my meal that I had information from an orderly room wallah that I was to report to Porton Down which was the Common Cold Research Establishment near Salisbury. It was something that I had forgotten all about. Every so often there would be a request on orders for volunteers to attend this establishment for fourteen days to act as guinea pigs. I think that there was a little incentive which was a few extra shillings on your pay. I believe this to be correct, but I am not absolutely sure. That may have been the reason for me to volunteer. However, the old Service saying was "Never volunteer for anything" and I was soon to find out the reason for that very saying. I just about had time to get my breath before I was on my way again.

On my arrival at the establishment, I was welcomed with open arms. You will soon read the reason for this welcome. In short, I was like a lamb to the slaughter. Like the fool I was, I was going to allow my body to be experimented on. Of course, I was assured that it was all in a good cause.

At first was the inevitable injection; not one, but two. This was the second time within a year of joining the Service that I had had injections of which I knew nothing about, and, to my disgrace, I never ever asked what they were for. I felt under the weather within a few hours, but nothing too serious. It felt like the beginning of influenza.

"How do you feel?" I was asked.

I described my symptoms to the doctor.

"I think that we will have to speed things up a little" he said. He instructed me to take a bath, then to get out of the bath, not dry myself, and to stand by the open window. After that session I did feel pretty ill. As the saying goes "Never volunteer".

I do not know what I was given to combat the illness, but it was in tablet form. I did have a fairly high temperature, and it was during this period of my induced illness that I was subjected to another experiment.

"Stand by this screen, facing the opening." That was the orderly giving me instructions. He left the room, and for good reason.

I waited for a while and I soon wondered if it was some sort of Porton joke. I should have known better as humorous situations at Porton Down were in short supply. My nostrils began to tighten and dizziness came over me. I absented myself from that situation in seconds. The orderly had the audacity to rebuke me for not waiting for his instructions. I retired to my room to rest and collect my thoughts.

I had been five days at Porton and I decided, come what may, I would leave as soon as I possibly could. The person that I spoke to was not very sympathetic towards me and I had the impression that he was avoiding my questions. Then he tried to convince me that it would be best to stay and complete the full time. "Sleep on it, and we will discuss it further" he said.

After further consideration, I decided that I would leave that evening and bugger the consequences.

I was about fifty to sixty miles from Portsmouth. My home is a lot nearer than Hednesford and to catch a train from Salisbury to Portsmouth would be fairly easy.

Somehow I walked out of Porton full of nerves and with some trepidation, but I can assure you, with absolutely no regrets. I had surprised myself with the decision that I had made to leave there without permission.

On reaching my home, and after a good chat with my dear father explaining everything, not least the situation at Porton, we agreed that I had done the right thing in walking out. He did urge me to report back to Hednesford as soon as I could, and he added that I was to report back to him if I was in any trouble. He would carry the matter to our local MP. Good old Dad.

I had a very strong feeling that there would be repercussions on my return to Hednesford, and my feelings never let me down. I reported to the guardroom on my arrival. Being permanent staff on the station I happened to know the S.P. on duty.

"Have I been reported absent without leave?" I asked.

"Well not exactly, Pompey, but you are to report to the station adjutant tomorrow morning" he said.

I have always avoided trouble in my life, and I hardly slept that night wondering what the outcome would be. After my meeting with the 'adj', I had made up my mind that there would be no excuses from my side. I would just state the facts. I still had a severe cold, and what I could not understand was the reason for the weakness in my hands. It was very difficult for me to grasp anything.

"Well, you have been a stupid man, now, tell me everything, including the reason for going absent" I was asked.

This I did. He seemed interested in my account of the situation at Porton Down, and I think that he was a little sympathetic. I had been absent for little more than thirty-six hours and I did not expect to get off scot-free. I was quite happy to accept his punishment. "You will be confined to camp for four days" he said. In other words, jankers. More of a nuisance than a punishment really.

RAF DEBDEN

I had already heard prior to my meeting with the 'adj' that I had been posted to RAF Debden in Essex to start in fourteen days' time. I also had a week to clear the station, so in effect, I had virtually finished working at RAF Hednesford. I was not sorry to be leaving the station, but I was sorry to be leaving behind some good friends. Service life is like that and there is always the real knowledge that you will make new friends at your next station.

Debden, being a flying station, was situated in a rural area, but I lived in the day of sensible transport and I was able to catch a train to get within a few miles of my destination. I had to change at Audly End which was on the main line then; after alighting, walk one hundred yards across the station yard and a little steam train was ready to take you on. A little different now, don't you think?

The nearest point to Debden was Saffron Walden, a very nice county town. A short journey by rail, but a bit of a long walk from Audly End.

I telephoned the guardroom at Debden and, lo and behold, I had transport provided. On arrival at camp I was directed to transit billet. By now it was tea time and time to try the camp grub, and as airmen's food goes, it was quite good.

After tea I was back to what I thought was going to be a lonely transit billet in which I had dumped my kit an hour ago. I was the only occupant. However, on entering the billet I came upon three others, and I will name them. Ron Dobbs from Tintern, South Wales; Sid Wilder from Chelmsford, and Tony Kerrison from Halesworth, which is, I think, in Suffolk. We became friends at once.

I would like to take a little time to give a mention to Ron Dobbs.

Of all the many friends that I made in the Air Force, the most rewarding was my friendship with Ron. Many hours were spent on shift together. We shared the same interests and we came from very similar backgrounds. A more honest and down-to-earth man I have yet to meet. To this day we have always been in touch with each other and our families have had many holidays together. I am very proud of the fact that we have been friends for nearly fifty years. I am sure many similar friendships were formed. I suppose one might say it was one of the more positive aspects of National Service.

The three of us were to work together in the officers' mess. RAF Debden officers' mess is a brick building built in the 1930s with a really nice frontage. The reception area was situated in the centre of the building, with the anteroom, dining room, bar and ladies' room adjacent within a few yards of the main entrance. Corridors were either side of the reception and they branched off and led to the officers' quarters, and very nice single rooms they were. Of course, the kitchens, servery, storerooms, offices, boiler house, staff room and sleeping quarters, were all to the rear of the building. In all a very nice little building. This pattern had been established and many messes all over the country were built to this design.

WAR MEMORIES
Debden had been a front line station in World War Two and some of the occupants had been the American Army Air Force. Stationed at Debden with the Americans was a very clever artist. He had done crayon portraits of the American officers stationed at Debden. They had been framed and hung on the walls of the main corridor. They were really wonderful pictures. I am not sure of this statement but maybe there were fifty or more of these portraits, and I have often wondered how many of these brave men survived the war. All of them, I hope.

In 1952, there were many American airmen stationed in East Anglia and they were always a good bet for a lift into London if they came your way. Very often they would be invited to a mess dance and they would never fail to be courteous to us waiters. Offers of drinks would come our way, which we had to refuse as we were on duty and not allowed to indulge. I think the portraits of their countrymen, which I mentioned earlier, made them feel very proud. And why not? I have always considered the Americans a good ally to this country.

In earlier pages, I mentioned briefly the Falklands War. What I have to tell you is that Debden was a training camp for aircrew and they were at Debden on various courses; e.g., navigation and other aspects of flying. Quite often Air Force officers from other countries would be taking the same course training as British officers. One course that I remember had many Argentinians on it and they probably passed on the knowledge that they had gained in England ready for future wars against England!! We were also training with men from Iraq. Need I say more?

Onto a more cheerful subject. It has been my good fortune in life to meet a lot of very nice people and, once again, as at my other postings, it was a pleasure to work with some very pleasant civilians; notably in the kitchens. There was a really first-class chef, a Mr Martin; his assistant cooks Danny Marsh and George Cornell, and not to forget the kitchen porter, Tom.

A mess of this size, with possibly a hundred living-in officers, would employ approximately fifteen civilians, and it has been my privilege to have known and worked with them. If Danny Marsh should, by chance, read this, then he won't mind me mentioning his new car.

It was his weekend on duty and it happened to be my shift. At tea break, there was a bit of a buzz in the air.

"Have you seen Danny's new car?" someone said.

"No, but I will have a look" was the reply.

It was a current model of a Triumph Mayflower. Now I know that this may seem like trivia or a nonevent to you, but remember that this was 1953 and for me to own a car was beyond my wildest dreams. Even more, I never had a clue about engines, and holding a driving licence was but a pipe dream. I felt a bit of envy, but I did not begrudge him this luxury. He had served in the Eighth Army on desert warfare and in Italy had had a very tough time indeed. In my eyes he had earned his bit of luxury, and I was very pleased for him.

I had two good reasons to remember that weekend. The car was the first and here goes with the second reason.

It was not always the lot of batmen/waiters to have living quarters within the officers' mess, but it was our luck at Debden to have this privilege, and luckily a code of practice was followed by the direction of the P.M.C. It was as follows: Living-in officers were instructed not to bother any member of off-duty staff, which was usually adhered to by the officers. However, my partner and I, Ron Dobbs, had completed our duties and we were in our quarters listening to Radio Luxembourg, when an officer entered the room. In a very polite manner he asked us if we would mind lighting a fire in a fellow officer's room. He would be returning from leave in the early hours of the morning and would appreciate this service. Nothing wrong with that request. What I haven't explained is, that to cope with the number of officers living-in, an annexe of wooden billets that were adjacent to the mess, were being used as an overflow. These buildings followed the familiar pattern, with a corridor down the centre of the building with rooms leading off. This was a 9' x 9' room with a combustion stove at one end. It was this 'horror' that we had to light. Anyone who is familiar with this type of stove will know that a good steady flow of air was the only way for this particular appliance to keep burning. Too much air or too little air flow and out it went. But Ron and I, old hands at this through experience, had the thing burning merrily away. As I have stated, it was unusual to be called whilst off duty, but, unexpectedly, there were two new arrivals to the mess, and it was our lot to provide them with rooms, help with luggage, and provide them with some sort of meal. Being involved in this type of situation, time passes quickly and your mind is concentrated entirely on the matter in hand.

Two hours has passed by and the time came for Ron and I to relax with a brew before turning in. But that was not to be!!

Ron to Mick, Mick to Ron, simultaneously: "THE BLOODY FIRE!!!"

In no time we were entering the end of the annexe. The room that we were making for was about halfway down the corridor, some fifty feet, and at once we could feel the heat. I grabbed the door handle. First mistake. It was too hot to hold so I doused the handle with water from the fire bucket. Looking back at this situation, I believe that this was the first time that I had ever seen water in a fire bucket during my Service.

Inside, the room was like a furnace. How it did not combust on our opening of the door, I shall never know. The actual stove and about two feet of the fuel pipe was glowing red-hot. The lino adjacent to the concrete stand in which the stove stood was bubbling.

The side of the bed cover nearest the stove was scorched, as was the wall behind the stove. Even the poker was too hot to hold without covering our hands.

We closed both flaps, top and bottom, to prevent air flow. Who thought of that I shall never know, but it worked. After a very worrying time the room cooled down and, much to our relief, the stove lost its glow. We replaced the bed cover, but we could do nothing about the burnt lino and scorched wall. However, all was not lost. Ron and I made sure that the room would be habitable for the pilot officer's return.

By now, midnight, we were ready to turn in and wonder what the repercussions would be in the morning. Sergeant Easton was the mess steward and he decided, after hearing our explanation, that it was just an unfortunate situation that needed no further action. We will never understand how the whole annexe did not burst into flames, but some sergeants would have punished us for what might have been.

By a strange coincidence, the building, the very same annexe, was severely damaged by fire about six weeks later and the circumstances were almost identical to a West End farce. It was lunch time and the mess was in full swing when a cloud of smoke engulfed the building. Someone had already summoned the station fire brigade. "Oh, that's alright then, everything under control." Not so. The fire brigade arrived OK and in quick time, but the most important piece of equipment was not on board the fire tender, notably the stopcock key.

The fire station headquarters was at the other end of the camp. The tender was surrounded by hoses and other fire equipment and so could not be moved at once. Some poor erk was sent for, at the treble, to collect a stopcock key. Well, of course, this farcical situation helped the fire along very nicely and the fear was that the adjacent annex would be lost as well. The officers were out of their billets and happily there was no risk of any personnel being injured. A great deal of officers' personal belongings were lost. I have no idea of the outcome regarding claims, etc., or of the enquiry that was to follow.

PROMOTION

I had risen from AC2 up to the dizzy heights of an LAC. Batmen/waiters were not classed as a technical trade, which meant that the rank of SAC could not be obtained. Right out of the blue I was asked how I would feel about being considered for promotion to corporal. I was very pleased as well as surprised, and I had no hesitation in saying that I would like to be considered. My interview was to be with the Catering Officer Flight Lieutenant Carey. I was a little nervous and, it turned out, I was on a short list of three candidates.

The outcome was to my satisfaction and after a couple of days I was making a journey to the stores to draw my chevrons two bar. I was pleased, and so was my father. My income rose to about £3.10s per week; a considerable sum at that time.

Perhaps this is a good time to make comparisons. I am not certain of these figures, but I believe at this time that a National Service pilot officer would have earned about £5 per week. Out of this amount he would have to pay mess bills. He would also be expected to buy his mess kit for special occasions, pay for footwear repairs and other expenses appertaining to officer status. So I feel sure that some would have been feeling the pinch on just a fiver a week. In comparison my wage was reasonable. I would have no outlay for food, etc. Rules and regulations, being what they are in the Services, meant that I had to have my own living quarters; in other words I was not allowed to live-in with the other ranks.

Never mind, one could never win them all!

IN AT THE DEEP END

Duty corporal was to be my new and next experience and, as it transpired, would have a lasting effect on my understanding of life and its meanings.

Standing orders at this time regarding air crashes were as follows: The nearest RAF station of the crash had to supply a crash guard, for obvious reasons. Just my luck to be orderly corporal! The station orderly officer was obliged to find four men and an NCO. I was the orderly corporal of the day and so it had to be me. A crash had occurred and Debden was the nearest station. In a very short time transport and our equipment (tents etc.) were made ready and we were on our way.

On arrival at the scene of the crash, we were given information regarding the crash. The police were already on the scene. The aircraft had crashed in a field, killing the pilot and his navigator. Pieces of the aircraft and parts of these poor airmen were placed on sacking in the tents that we had erected. These were ready for the boffins from Farnborough to inspect.

Our little group stood guard throughout the night until 1p.m. the next day. We were relieved and quite pleased to be on our way back to Debden.

Sadly though, it was not the end of the matter as far as I was concerned. The funerals of the aircrew had to be arranged, and the service would be conducted at Debden. As senior batman/waiter I had to make ready the visitors' room to receive the parents of the deceased. I also had to be in attendance.

The memory of this day remains firmly in my mind. It was a bleak, snow-flurried February day. I had made ready tea, coffee, and alcoholic drinks were also available. Everything possible was done to ease the pain that these people must have been feeling. The parents duly arrived and they actually went out of their way to make me feel at ease, and yet they were the ones suffering. I was asked by one of the mothers if I had written letters to my parents on a regular basis, and I had to admit that I hadn't. She urged me to give this some consideration. She was the mother of the pilot, a young man of twenty-three years. She said that she would have loved him to have written more often to her and, again, she urged me to write more often to my parents.

That day, and what that sad lady said to me, made me realise how important parents are. I think that it is a sad fact that young people spend very little time talking to their parents.

I had had quite a week as a newly-promoted corporal, but I had learned a great deal from a very tragic event.

OFFICERS' LADIES

A weekly event at the mess at Debden was the officers' wives coffee afternoon. The ladies' room was always used for this purpose. Fancy cakes baked by the chef were provided and little triangle-shaped sandwiches, with the crust off, prepared by yours truly.

Before being promoted to corporal, it depended what shift you were on whether you were involved with this particular event. But the commanding officer's wife attended these events and so the mess secretary insisted that a corporal be in attendance. This I did not mind one bit, as it was an easy number. What I could never understand was the reason that they were so rank-conscious. Senior officers' wives would be together and junior officers' wives congregated in another part of the room. The real lady that stood out like a beacon was the commanding officer's wife. Her husband was a group captain and an ex-Battle of Britain pilot. She did her best to pull this lot together, but it was an uphill task. She could have pulled rank on all of them, if she so wished. She had seen life in the Service on a war footing and realised the futility of upmanship.

I had worked in officers' married quarters and, believe me, some of them could have had lessons in cleanliness and good housekeeping. The idea of a batman working in officers' married quarters, was to supply a service to the officer; looking after his uniform, etc. But on many instances you were looked upon as a skivvy by the officer's wife, and very often, when reporting for duty, you would be presented with a list of chores. For example: peel the potatoes, clean the windows, make the beds, wash-up the breakfast china, etc. In short you were treated as a general dogsbody. And, of course, the lady of the house would have the full support of her husband in this situation, and to hell with regulations.

An AC1 batman/waiter did rebel and refused to do household chores. Surprisingly he was returned to duties in the mess. Maybe not so surprising? His stand against this waste of manpower, and being taken advantage of, benefited all of us. No longer did we have the imposition of household chores thrust upon us.

National Service was introduced for this reason.

Myself and some good friends, RAF Debden, 1953

COMMITMENT

My time on shiftwork at Debden allowed me to go home every other weekend, if I so wished. In spite of being away from home, I had no wish to lose contact with my friends in civvy street.

In Portsmouth at this time (the early fifties), places of entertainment, i.e. dance halls, theatres, cinemas and youth clubs, were in abundance; so for an evening out there was always an excellent choice. Very often you would meet an old friend doing his National Service and also home on leave.

If I arrived home in time for an evening out, usually on a Friday evening, I would make my way from Milton Road down to the Spread Eagle public house in Arundel Street. That good old pub was a meeting point for our gang, and I was always sure of making contact with my friends. If, by chance, my friends had gone on to the venue for the evening's entertainment, then Edna, who ran the pub with Auntie, would always be able to point me in the right direction. "Vic Spry, John Potter, Kenny Atkins told me to tell you that they would be at the Savoy in Southsea. It's Radio Big Band Night" she would say.

Another favourite venue for us at this time was the Labour Club in St John's Road, Fratton. It was only a 1/6d hop, but we always seemed to enjoy it. It was at one of these hops that I met my wife to be. Her name was June Bundy. After a number of meetings we thought that getting engaged to be married would be a good idea, and so it was.

An event such as this opens up new horizons, and during my time away from June, I never thought of much else, apart from my next leave when I could be with her.

I always hitchhiked home and always caught the train back to camp. I think that I am right in saying that to any ex-serviceman, a forty-eight hour pass seemed like one day or less, and I always waited until the last minute before making my way to the train station. I could have caught an earlier train than the 10.25 to Waterloo, which would have made getting back to Debden a whole lot easier, but newly engaged airmen did not think like that.

The train reached Waterloo at midnight and I had to be at Liverpool Street station for the 1.30 train to Audly End. Lots of time to spend on draughty and cold Liverpool Street station. As usual the waiting room would be closed and there was absolutely no chance of a warm drink. A bit like now, I suppose. But ladies of the night would be there in abundance, plying their wares to all and sundry. At about 2.15 a.m., the train would stop at Audly End, but at this time of the morning you could not reach Saffron Walden by connecting train. Fortunately an enterprising coach operator would carry you to Debden for one shilling. Even at that time of the morning, more often than not, the coach would be filled, and that included people standing in the aisle. Everyone returning from leave and all as miserable as sin!

I was one of the lucky ones, as a flask of tea or coffee would be provided from whoever was on duty in the mess, although not officially, of course! We provided this little service for each other, and it was fully appreciated. It could be very cold in that part of the world.

Why catch the very last train to have to go through all this hassle when an earlier train would have made travelling back so much easier? I think that I was in love!

CLOSE ENCOUNTER OF THE WRONG KIND

I suppose that any narrative of this nature, written at this time, would include the subject of homosexuality. The questions likely to be asked would be "Did they exist in the Services?" and "Were they a problem?" Happily, I never experienced this type of situation at any time during my Service, but I will tell you of an experience that I had, without being directly involved.

Another airman and I were duty shift at a very quiet time of the year. Seventy per cent of the officers had taken their annual leave which, of course, from our point of view, was wonderful. It was a time for us waiters to relax, but we still had to fulfil duty shifts. During the serving of dinner, I was asked by a squadron leader if it would be possible for his after dinner coffee to be served in his room.

"Of course Sir, but you may have to wait for a convenient moment" I told him.

"That's OK. Bring it to my room when you are ready" he said.

It never occurred to me to even imagine why he could not carry his own coffee to his room, but I suppose that, without knowing it, we were being conditioned into pampering these privileged people.

The two of us on shift decided that we would take his coffee to his room after we had eaten our evening meal, and then that would be the end of our duties for the day.

"I'll take the lazy sod's coffee if you will make a cup of tea" said Sid.

"OK, Sid" I replied. "It's a deal."

I never realised it at the time, but agreeing to Sid's suggestion would save me from being in a very embarrassing situation. However, poor old Sid was not to be saved from this!

"I've poured the tea" I said, with my back to the staff room door, as Sid returned from taking the squadron leader his coffee.

"That dirty bastard!!" exclaimed Sid.

I turned around and noticed at once that Sid was in a flaming rage.

"Calm down" I said, "you are not making sense at the moment." I never imagined what it could be that had made Sid so angry.

He then began to explain. "I knocked the door and entered the room, after he had told me to enter. The senior officer was lying on top of the bed completely unclothed." In Service language "Bollock naked".

"What I would really like is for you to massage me all over. I am sure that you could" said the officer.

"Do you think he is a poofter?" I asked Sid.

"I know damn well he is" replied Sid, "and what's more I am going to stop his bloody game right now."

"Don't do anything that you might regret" I said. I knew full well that my fellow airman was a fiery character, and I could see the possibility of assault. "What are you going to do?" I asked Sid. I felt rather silly asking these seemingly inadequate questions.

"I am going to see the commanding officer" replied Sid.

"But Sid, it's 8 p.m. on a Sunday evening, you can't barge in on him at his married quarters" I said.

"You bloody well watch me" was Sid's reply.

And that is just what he did. He was back within the hour. "I am to report to his office in the morning. I think that he was a bit surprised to see me" said Sid. (I bet he was.) Sid continued "I am sorry Mick, but you are ordered to report with me."

"Don't worry about that Sid, I will," I replied, "and I'll back you all the way."

Brave words. The squirming and lying of this officer had to be seen to be believed. I could understand my pal's frustration, and the situation became very heated. In a very strange way I began to feel sorry for the C.O., as I had always considered him to be a decent man, which he was. As far as I know the only outcome was a posting for the officer.

I have often wondered if I would have reacted in the same way as my friend had, and I think that the answer to that would be yes.

RIGHT MARKER

It was usually excepted on RAF stations that officers' mess staff would not be required for parades and guard duties. It is not as unfair to other staff as it may seem. As a matter of course, officers' mess staff would be on duty well before most other sections, and would be required to work in the mess for many other functions, such as dances, dining-in nights, ladies' night, etc., etc., even when officially off shift.

As is often the case in many walks of life, someone will want to alter a system that is already working well, and it was to be the case at Debden. A new station adjutant was feeling his wings. Commanding officer's parade was held every two weeks and normally this parade would not affect the mess staff, but this new broom insisted that officers' mess staff were to be included. I had this information (or gen) from a fellow corporal in the station warrant officer's office, well before the parade state was announced. One of the advantages of being a corporal.

The routine for this parade was for all ranks to assemble on the perimeter and make ready for the parade proper, and to be there at 08.00 hours sharp. Not much in that I hear you say, and you are quite right, but work in the officers' mess is a little different from other sections. Breakfast would start being served at 07.00, but many officers, being on all kinds of aircrew training courses, would commence work at varying times, and breakfast times tended to drag on. A big percentage of our workforce was required for C.O.'s parade and, as a result of this, many officers either had to wait for breakfast, which made them late, or miss breakfast altogether. They were not happy men.

Happily or unhappily, I was not in attendance during the chaos,

I had to be on parade. I was all 'bulled up' and milling around on the perimeter, when I was called over to the 'swoman'.
"Corporal Franckeiss you will be right marker" he said.
"Please Sir, I would rather die," I felt like saying. 'How do I get out of this one?' The fact that I was a corporal gave the SWO the idea that I would be able to perform the duties of a right marker. Parading with rifles was an art in itself, but to do the duties of a right marker, for me, was out of the question. I had to think of something or it would be 'worm's eye view' all over again. I never had any ammunition, so shooting myself in the foot was out of the reckoning. My only option was to own up and bugger the consequences. But I had better hurry as fall in time was very near. I marched ten yards over to the SWO with a great deal of trepidation. I came to attention in front of him. 'Here goes,' I thought to myself, 'stand by for a good bollocking.' "Excuse me Sir" I said.
He looked at me as if I had just crawled from under a stone. "Well, get on with it. What do you want?" he said.
"I have to tell you Sir, that I have never done right marker" I replied. That is all that I managed to say before the tirade began.
At the top of his voice he bellowed "So you can't do right marker. Are you in the bloody Air Force or not?" Of course, the whole parade could hear every word. "What section do you work in?" he asked.
"Officers' mess Sir" I replied.
"Well that explains everything; you are in a world of your own. Aren't you? Get back in to line and report to me after the parade" was his reply.
So far so good. Parade over and I did as I was told. He had cooled off by this time and even called me 'laddie'. The truth was I had not paraded with a rifle since my square-bashing days, and I think that he understood the predicament that I was in.
An RAF Regiment section was on the station and I had to report to them for drill instruction. I saw no need to argue with this, as I had got off very lightly. A warrant officer did not mess in a commissioned officer's mess, but he would in a sergeant's mess, and that was the reason that he would not have known me.

INTO BATTLE

Any ex-serviceman reading this will be familiar with manoeuvres. This is when other ranks are to wear camouflage gear, black their faces, carry a .303 Lee Enfield rifle, creep around in the pitch-black and try to be as much like the real thing as possible.

Now I don't know much about the Army officers when on manoeuvres, but I do know where you would find an RAF officer after the word to go was given. There is a strong possibility that he would be in the mess entertaining the umpires. The umpires are the people who tell you if you are dead!

Just for a bit of variety, I suppose, these manoeuvres on this occasion would involve the Army. That made us feel a lot better, knowing that the squaddies would lose a night's sleep as well as us.

During the activity, the officers' mess had to stay open; therefore two waiters had to be in attendance to serve drinks, etc. The two waiters were me and one other.

"A cushy little number" I hear you say. How right you are. If I had to be on duty, which, of course, I had to be, why not spend my time in a nice warm mess, instead of running around in the dark with someone firing blanks at you?

The idea of this particular exercise, was for the Army to 'capture' RAF Debden and our 'brave lads' were to stop this happening.

So the battle raged; well, I heard plenty of bangs and my colleague and I were serving drinks nonstop. What a battle we had! We ran short of glasses twice. After about three hours of this farce, a little of the excitement came our way. This was 'real' action. I was pouring yet more tea when I 'blacked up'. A squaddie burst into the kitchen, ordered me to stand still, and told me that I was under arrest. For the moment I imagined that my future mother-in-law had joined the Army, and this was her way of preventing me from marrying her daughter.

I carried on pouring the tea, that's how brave I am!

Again he shouted "Stand still, you are under arrest."

"OK, OK. Do you want a cup of tea or not?" I replied to him.

I thought that he was going to explode. "I am going outside to call the umpire and you are coming with me" he exclaimed.

"Oh for Christ's sake, sit down and have a drink" I fumed, as by this time I was quite pissed off.

Still he ranted on. "I am not going anywhere" he insisted and then (and this cheered me up no end), "you are just not playing the game properly."

Was I hearing things? 'Well,' I thought, 'if we are going to play silly buggers then I may just as well join in.' Noticing that he was a lance corporal, and me being a full corporal, I decided to pull rank, just for the devil of it to see what his reaction would be.

On noticing this, he changed from a battling warrior into a seemingly forlorn creature, almost at once. "You're just not interested" he said, and I do believe that he was sincere. He simply left the mess and went on to manoeuvre somewhere else. I suppose that it takes all kinds, but I was just not interested in war games, especially at that time of the morning!

I think that I could consider that battle experience! Just about enough for my needs.

LET ME OUT

I think that the way that a lot of National Servicemen saw their stint in the RAF was as something that had to be done, and, therefore, take the view that it was best to just get on with it, and hope that two years would pass by very quickly, or if you had the nerve and the persistence, try and work your ticket.

A man with the latter idea in mind arrived to work in the mess and he had only recently completed square-bashing, so he was probably feeling disillusioned with Service life, even at this early stage. I could put a name to this man, but it would serve no purpose; I will just call him Jack.

A good many personnel were posted directly to what was to be their permanent posting and on-the-job training was a normal procedure. As a senior rank working in the mess, I would be involved in the batmen/waiters-to-be training. I usually enjoyed this part of my job as it was a nice change to my normal working day.

That was the situation until Jack came along; I think just to make things a little different. Either he could not, or would not, grasp the simplest of explanations or instructions. Try as I might it became an impossible task to teach him anything at all.

The mess steward did find work for him in the mess, but it had to be in the wash-up. He was on the camp strength as an AC2 and he came up on orders for fire picket duty. I did my best to explain to him what his duties entailed. In short, if the camp siren was operated, then personnel who were on fire picket detail, should report to the fire station as quickly as possible.

Well, men being what they are, would ask Jack if he had heard the siren and, of course, more often than not, it hadn't been sounded, but nevertheless Jack still bounded off to the fire station, only to be told that the alarm had not been activated.

I think that Jack cottoned on to this situation. He didn't respond at all, genuine or not. I think, personally, that Jack had secretly put 'stage two' into operation.

'Stage three' was a little different. Any normal serviceman would know that if a limousine-type vehicle, flying a pennant, happened to come by, then it would be policy to salute. The chances are that the vehicle would not be carrying an officer, but salute anyway. Not Jack!

This happened to him, not once, but twice, when he was walking through the camp.

"Come here Airman" said a voice.

The car had stopped. Jack walked to the car, didn't stand to attention and didn't salute. When being questioned he leaned into the car window, maybe to have a cosy chat with the officer. He got a good bollocking, of course.

On other occasions, when a similar thing happened, nobody would take any notice. Jack was making a name for himself around the camp, and it looked as if 'stage three' of his plan was a success as well.

Jack seemed to come out of his shell a little bit more, and during the course of conversation, mentioned that his sister was getting married in the near future. It was suggested by some joker that he should apply for a Service marriage allowance, never dreaming that Jack would do so, but maybe Jack saw this as another opportunity to discredit himself, and therefore enhance his chances, still further, of an early release.

A friend of mine happened to be a corporal in the pay office and I told him that Jack would soon be paying him a visit in his office to claim a marriage allowance for his sister's forthcoming marriage.

He laughed, of course, our Jack was becoming very well known all over Debden and the corporal played along with this weird scenario.

I suspect that Jack would be laughing even longer!!

There were many times that little episodes such as this were the talking point of the camp staff, including officers, I might add.

On another memorable occasion, he asked the medical officer to give him something to stop moths sleeping in his bed!!

Determination was one of our Jack's strong points. To give him his due, he stuck to his task and eventually waved goodbye to us. I say a wave, but it could just have likely to have been two fingers stuck up in the air. Whatever it was, I did secretly admire him. If ever he were to read this he would know who that character was at Debden, who gave everyone so much pleasure!

DEMOB AT LAST

Well folks, this is to be the final chapter. I finally had the great pleasure of marking off the penultimate week of my Service. Any ex-National Serviceman reading this will be familiar with the good old demob wall chart that many had hanging above their beds. We would religiously tick the weeks, days and even the hours of these; sometimes, works of art.

At this time, corporals and above, in rank, were required by the C.O. to attend an interview if that person was about to be demobbed. The reason for this I was about to find out very shortly. He tried, in a friendly way, to persuade me to stay in the Service. I must be truthful and say that he had some very good points to make. He indicated that I would be promoted to sergeant within two years and for a man of my limited education that would have been a fair achievement! He also asked me if I was married, and when I replied that I was about to, he said that I would be granted married quarters and, therefore, in a stroke, solve the problem of finding accommodation for my new wife and myself. "What are the prospects when you return to the building trade in civvy street?" he asked, and I had to say nil.

On reflection, I cannot believe that I actually turned down this good offer of security for the foreseeable future. At the time all that was in my mind was demob, and I did not give enough consideration as to what was on offer. Quite honestly, in my case anyway, it was the awful thought of being at the beck and call of some of those ex-university prattish junior officers.

In one's life, I firmly believe that at some time a person will make a wrong decision on an important issue, and I now know that I had made the wrong decision when I decided to leave the Royal Air Force.

I feel sure that my decision to leave the Royal Air Force was influenced by the fact that I had become engaged to be married to my beloved June, and after each leave that I had enjoyed with my future wife it had become more difficulty to say goodbye. I had made the silly mistake of not considering being married whilst still serving, which would, of course, solved housing and employment instantly, and my prospects, I feel sure, would have been much brighter than the building trade that I was going back to in civvy street.

It could have been the fact that I, like many others, had been forced into something, and perhaps, subconsciously, I was looking for a bit of revenge by saying 'I am leaving, whatever you say, so up yours!' I will say in all honesty that I have no regrets at having served in the RAF. It was my good fortune to meet some very fine people from all walks of life, civilians as well as servicemen, and it made one realise and appreciate what a good home was being left behind when entering the Service.

I have no wish to prattle on about discipline, etc., etc., only to say that it is sadly lacking in our society today, and I firmly believe that a stint in the Services can do nothing but good in the building of any character.

In closing I would like to wish all those ex-servicemen of the forties and fifties, whom most, I feel sure, are now grandads, all the very best in the world, and I feel certain that they have some good memories of some good friends.

THE END

RAF Debden Demob Party